Life-Changing Faith For Today

Why Luther's Theology Still Matters

David J. Monge

Foreword by Martin E. Marty

CSS Publishing Company, Inc., Lima, Ohio

LIFE-CHANGING FAITH FOR TODAY

Unless marked otherwise scriptures are from the *Revised Standard Version of the Bible*, copyrighted 1946, 1952 ©, 1971, 1973, by the Division of Christian Education of the National Council of the Churches of Christ in the USA. Used by permission.

Scripture quotations marked (NRSV) are from the *New Revised Standard Version of the Bible*, copyright 1989 by the Division of Christian Education of the National Council of the Churches of Christ in the USA. Used by permission.

Library of Congress Cataloging-in-Publication Data

Monge, David.
   Life-changing faith for today : why Luther's theology still matters / David J. Monge; foreword by Martin E. Marty.
     p. cm.
Includes bibliographical references.
   ISBN 0-7880-1948-1 (pbk. : alk. paper)
   1. Luther, Martin, 1483-1546. 2. Theology, Doctrinal—Popular works. I. Title.
BR333.3 M66 2003
230'.41'092—dc21

                                2002013720

For more information about CSS Publishing Company resources, visit our website at www.csspub.com or e-mail us at custserv@csspub.com or call (800) 241-4056.

ISBN 0-7880-1948-1
                                     PRINTED IN U.S.A.

For our
children
and
grandchildren

Table Of Contents

Author's Preface

This book grew out of my own interest in writing a brief introduction to the theology of Martin Luther for use with adult education groups and new members entering our congregation.

Thirty years of parish ministry experience have taught me that little is known of Luther's thought, both among those who have grown up in the Lutheran Church and among those who view us quizzically from the outside. Twenty-seven of those years were spent in the Midwest, where the Lutheran Church took root among Scandinavian and German immigrants. Older people there remembered hearing their parents and friends debating, often rather heatedly, the question of predestination at the turn of the twentieth century. These debates became so heated that families and congregations split apart. This may be one of the reasons why the issue was not talked about much as the new century advanced. A century ago, people at least knew what the debate was about and held strong opinions about it.

Following World War II, when I was born, the issue was never raised. Pelagianism (the notion that we must love God or, at the bare minimum, accept Jesus as our personal Lord and Savior before we could be saved) ruled the day and still does. This tradition has a long history, beginning with the British monk Pelagius, who lived in the fourth century A.D., and continuing through Erasmus of Rotterdam at the time of the Reformation and into contemporary evangelical Christianity, which has been the dominant voice of Protestantism in America. In this context, Luther's theology sounds alien, with its stress on God's election of us.

And yet, I recall that as I was growing up, I felt that something was frightfully wrong with the decision-for-Christ-theology that was being proclaimed in my home church and elsewhere. Somehow I knew that if it was up to me to accept and love God, I would never make it. How would I know if my decision for Jesus was sincere enough, given all the growing questions and doubts about

7

God that were forming in my young mind. On the one hand, I embraced the theology I was taught and even defended it vehemently on occasion. On the other hand, this theology sounded fundamentally flawed and wrong, although at that point I couldn't have said why.

I found myself adrift. By the time I had finished my university studies, I wanted little to do with the Christian Church, but found myself drawn to the study of theology, nonetheless. My advisor was Edmund Smits, who had come to the United States as a refugee from Latvia after the Communist takeover of that country after World War II. He listened patiently to my doubts and questions and wisely steered me in the direction of Luther's theology. I didn't take to it right away. It still seemed alien. My studies at Luther Theological Seminary in St. Paul, Minnesota, particularly with professors Roy Harrisville in New Testament studies and Gerhard Forde in systematic theology opened Luther's world of thought in all its strange beauty, and I knew that, like a latter day prodigal son, I had returned home at last and was seeing it, really, for the first time. This book is an attempt to describe this strange beauty, however partial it no doubt is.

I wish to take this opportunity to thank my teachers at Luther Theological Seminary: Edmund Smits, who died a decade ago, whom many of us knew affectionately as "Papa," Roy Harrisville and Gerhard Forde, who opened up for so many of us the theology of Luther, and my classmate and dear friend, Jim Nestingen, who has seen me through some very tough times. And I wish to thank the members of my parishes in North Dakota, Minnesota, and California, who have listened to me preach and teach over the past three decades. You have been a wonderful source of love, acceptance, and nurture to me. I suspect that I have learned much more from you, than you have from me, about the art of daily living.

Most of all, thanks to my wife, Pamela McCrea, who continues to be my dearest friend. You have taught me how to live in and to love the present moment, and for that I will be eternally grateful.

David J. Monge
Huntington Beach, California
St. Valentine's Day, 2002

Foreword

At the end of the second millennium, when makers of lists pursued the question of who were the most important people in the thousand years past, Martin Luther, a man at their mid-point, regularly showed up near the top. Whoever tackles bibliographies and catalogues in libraries will find him up there with Jesus, Napoleon, and Abraham Lincoln among the most written about. While the Reformation was many things, based on incidents that occurred two centuries before Luther and expressed in parallel events with which he had little or nothing to do, ask most people about the Reformation and they start talking about Luther.

Ask people about the ideas of Luther and matters grow somewhat more confused. Before the Second Vatican Council (1962–1965) only sophisticated historians among Roman Catholics were taught to think well of him. The average layperson and the priest down the block inherited traditions of suspicion and condemnation. In the secular academy you would get good answers about Luther as a cultural figure, but few penetrated his theological ideas. In East Germany, when a-theists ruled, he was portrayed as a liberator, a man of the people, an educator, but never as theologian. In the American religious world, most people would have heard of him, but what did they know and think?

If you follow the traces you will find Luther's fan club speaking extravagantly in praise of his achievements. He gets credited for inventing modern political freedom. He didn't. One would think that he invented the Boy Scouts, the United States Constitution, and the public schools. He did not come close to the themes to which they are devoted.

A figure as explosive — as much given to speaking in terms that seem to contradict each other, and often do — as we find Luther to have been also awakens vicious critics for sub-themes in his plot. While David J. Monge does not mention it, in contemporary

9

historical and political circles his well-known anti-Semitism, expressed in what have come to be embarrassing terms that should always have been seen as scandalous, gets most attention. Religious radicals portray him as a lackey, a bootlicker to the establishment who licensed priests to kill peasants. Some modern feminists fault him for not being devoted to causes that animate the National Organization for Women. In other words, he is denigrated for being a sixteenth-century person. Seldom would his theological ideas come up in these contexts.

Listen to evangelicals who like him and you will hear him portrayed as a supporter of "biblical inerrancy." Wrong again. He believed in the full authority of the Bible, and would take no doctrines that were not, in his mind, clearly anticipated in the scriptures. But he was not much given to making things come out right when a Gospel writer makes a wrong citation, when the author of Esther forgets to mention God, when the Epistle of James does not promote grace. For him, Christ was the center of the Scriptures, which were a kind of manger that held him. Still, people are not off track when they cite the "scripture alone" theme as something in the Luther package.

Of course, Luther comes off as an individualist, a kind of libertarian, in many American accounts. Not on your life, nor in his. Pastor Monge quotes the *Large Catechism* to show how "churchly" and communal Luther's thought was. He would have little room for people who "love Jesus but hate the church," who are "spiritual but not religious" (though Monge shows that Luther would not have found most definitions of "religion" congenial either).

Get close to Luther, as writers of books of doctrine did a century after he lived, and you get the impression that he taught a sequence of truths. Bishop Einar Billing a century ago contended properly that Luther's teaching is not "doctrines" like pearls on a string (cut the string, take one out, tie it up, and you are almost where you were). No, you will never understand a serious and extended thought of Luther about the Christian message unless it can somehow be reduced to a corollary of the gospel of the forgiveness of sins. More simply stated: Think of that gospel of forgiveness (= "justification by grace through faith," more precisely, as in this book) as the glowing core out of which heat radiates, or the sun which has illuminating rays that "go out" if the sun is obscured.

Pastor Monge is convinced that Luther has not yet been introduced or caught onto in America, and has written this book to help the cause along, a cause that reaches for that "justification by faith" theme. I am an American religious historian, not a chauvinist for whom America can do no wrong. But I think he is a bit hard on America. He thinks "we" don't know Luther at all; he has not reached our shores. I'd be gentler with three centuries of Lutheran preachers and congregations on these shores, and on many evangelical teachers from 1607 to 2001. Or, to put it another way, I would not suggest that his gospel was caught on to all that much in Europe. Did Iceland, Denmark, Sweden, Norway, Finland, or the Lutheran parts of Germany get it right? Billing thought them "slack," and said there was nothing more slack than slack Lutheranism.

Monge is correct: teaching "justification by faith" is concentrating on a rather simple reality that gets blurred and muddied not because we who hear it are stupid but because we like to hang on to our own efforts and achievements, and these compromise the direct address of a justifying God to our situation.

That is why he wrote this book. He is not pretending to be adding one more work about which the scholars should fight. He is out to reach those who welcome growth, who have curiosity, who wish to grow in faith, and want to use Luther's life and teaching as a prism through which to view the Christian reality. As a former pastor in a congregation who knows how consuming pastoral work is, I've always both applauded pastors and chaplains who write and marveled that some do. Pastor Monge is widely read and draws on a considerable range of literature, when that is appropriate. He does not introduce the names of others to impress readers but because they reinforce the major themes.

So, in the world crowded with books, few of which teach "justification by faith," this work enters a field and bids for readers, people whose lives stand a chance of being changed by "theology" that, in the subtitle of this book, "still matters." I would perhaps have changed it — if one buys the thesis that the teaching has not sufficiently caught on, and recognizing that it is ahead of us — to "Why Luther's Theology Matters Already."

Martin E. Marty
The Fairfax M. Cone Distinguished
    Service Professor Emeritus
The University of Chicago

Introduction

Who Cares About Theology?

Theology Is The Church's Responsibility

In 1994, at the close of his formal career as a teacher of theology, theologian George Forell wrote:

> *If the church abandons its responsibility to theology to devote itself entirely to entertainment, pop-psychology, and social work, the task of helping people with the big questions will be assumed by others. If that happens, somebody will eventually write a book with the title,* The Treason of the Church.
>
> *It was at that point in a very similar condition almost 500 years go that Luther entered the picture. At the end of my pilgrimage I am convinced that his relevance to our situation is enormous.*[1]

American Christians, to a great degree, have abandoned theology. Theology, the careful thinking about Scripture and tradition, is regarded as nonessential to faith. We hear it said quite regularly that what one believes isn't important. What is important is that one believes *something*. The Reformers encountered something similar in the church 500 years ago. There was plenty of belief, but it had precious little to do with the Bible. Moreover, what people were being taught to believe was not innocent — that is, some of it was destructive of life itself.

After all, to believe or to have faith means to trust. Atheism, strictly speaking, isn't possible for human beings, because we all place our trust in someone or something. In the *Large Catechism* Luther asks:

> *What is it to have a god? Answer: A god is that to which we look for all good and in which we find refuge in*

13

*every time of need. To have a god is nothing else than
to trust and believe him with our whole heart. As I have
often said, the trust and faith of the heart alone make
both God and an idol. If your faith and trust are right,
then your God is the true God. On the other hand, if
your trust is false and wrong, then you have not the
true God. For these two belong together, faith and God.
That to which your heart clings and entrusts itself is, I
say, really your God.*[2]

Today, September 11, 2001, as I put the finishing touches on
this manuscript, hijacked airliners have been flown into the World
Trade Center in New York City and the Pentagon in Washington,
D.C. Thousands of people are dead. The nation has been effec-
tively shut down. This massive destruction was caused by people
who believed very deeply in what they were doing. They believed
passionately enough to sacrifice their own lives, along with the
lives of thousands of American workers. What sort of system of
belief would require such an unspeakable act? What sort of god
were the destroyers serving? Belief is not innocent. It can be sadly
and tragically misguided. Perhaps it is time to examine the gods
we serve. Perhaps it is time once again to take theology seriously.

The Tower Of Babel: Symbol Of Our Age
Genesis 11 records the story of the tower of Babel. Human-
kind decided to build a tower that would reach into heaven itself.
By means of this tower human beings would take heaven by storm,
dethrone God, and become gods themselves. It was the "logical"
outcome of what the serpent had told Adam and Eve: "You will not
die [if you eat of the forbidden fruit]; for God knows that when
you eat of it your eyes will be opened, knowing good and evil"
(Genesis 3:4-5, NRSV). God saw what was happening and confused the language of the people, so that the building of the tower
had to be abandoned. Therefore the tower was called Babel, because God confused the languages of all the earth (Genesis 11:9).
Not all members of the same denomination believe the same
things. Listening to any group of Christians talk among themselves

14

suggests that there is a great deal of confusion about what they believe to be true. Although we may be surprised to discover this when we look into another church tradition from the outside, there is a great deal of disagreement within groups of Lutherans, Baptists, Presbyterians, Catholics, Methodists, and others over issues of belief and practice.

There was a time when it could be said that all Christians agreed on certain basics — otherwise they would not regard themselves as Christian. A recent survey done by the Barna Research Group in Ventura, California, however, found that two-thirds of the mainline Christians surveyed do not believe that Jesus is truly God. They think of Jesus as a moral teacher, like the Dalai Lama — someone to be admired. Moreover, the doctrine of the Trinity (that God is Father, Son, and Spirit) is up for grabs. We aren't at all sure any more what calling God triune means.

Spirituality is fascinating for many today, but there is no commonly accepted definition of what that word means. Perhaps it means abandoning the American Dream and moving into the desert to commune with the coyotes and cacti. Perhaps it means adopting a distinctive spiritual vocabulary of some kind that sets one apart from everyone else. It might mean adopting a certain style of music and worship. Often it means wanting nothing to do with institutionalized religion. It can, in fact, mean almost anything. In this regard, our time is very similar to the first century A.D. It, too, was an intensely religious time, when numerous faiths competed with one another for peoples' allegiance. Like ours, it was a time of disenchantment with traditions as well as time of searching for what can be regarded as true.

Neither is there any consensus about basic texts and how to understand and interpret them. Some Christians claim to read the Bible literally (as it is written), while others acknowledge that all reading of the Bible involves interpretation. And there is considerable disagreement on the matter of what constitutes authentic interpretation. Does the Bible contain contradictions? Are some of its teachings dated and no longer binding?

Some Christians are uncomfortable with the humanity of Jesus and would just as soon have him be only divine, because human nature is often messy and contradictory, while whatever is divine is pure and must not be tainted by contact with the world. Others, as the Barna Research Group discovered, are uncomfortable with the notion of Jesus as God. And the catalogue of disagreements goes on. It's a wonder that we can point to anything that Christians don't argue about, sometimes with great vehemence and even violence. At times in the 2,000-year history of the church, Christians have persecuted other Christians even to the point of killing one other. The history of the church, like the history of any other institution, is riddled with absurdities, hatreds, contradictions, and violence. It's surprising it has lasted as long as it has. More often than not, the church has resembled a derelict ship, always on the verge of sinking, battered by wind and waves, forever drifting off course, leaking oil, and coming apart at the seams.

Or, to change metaphors, it often resembles an asylum that has been taken over by the inmates. The bickering is enough to drive anyone crazy! So why take such a silly thing seriously? Why give it any credence at all? Better, perhaps, just to forget it — which many, both inside and outside the church, have done. One wag put it this way, "Jesus came preaching the kingdom of God, but ended up with the church instead." It's a bit like opening up a beautiful Christmas present only to discover a lump of coal inside the wonderful wrapping.

So why not just opt out, jump ship, climb the fence, kiss the whole miserable thing farewell? There are a thousand good reasons for doing so, reasons that apply to everything else in our common life — business, politics, education, the sciences, and all the rest of it. Of course, one expects disagreement and, often, bad behavior among politicians. The business world is a matter of the survival of the fittest and often resembles a war zone. Nothing heats up a discussion among rational people quite the way educational reform does. Even the sciences, those ventures that are dedicated to the pursuit of pure reason, become compromised by competition for funding and the need to be recognized. There doesn't even seem to be much agreement about how a work of literature or a piece of music should be interpreted.

It Wasn't Any Different In "The Good Old Days"

Supposedly, however, the church was meant to be above all that. Yet, if one reads the New Testament Gospels, it quickly becomes apparent that not even Jesus could keep twelve men happy. His disciples were forever bickering, disagreeing, and vying for attention, sometimes to the point of violence with each other and with the enemies of Jesus. In the Garden of Gethsemane, the night before Jesus was killed, one of his disciples took up the sword against a servant of one of those who came to arrest Jesus, cutting off the servant's ear (Matthew 26:51). And, when push came to shove, his disciples forsook him when he was arrested (Mark 14:50) and fled, more interested in saving their own skins than in standing by him.

The story told in the Gospels is not a pretty one. It is a story (like the Old Testament before it) of self-interest, cowardice, hatred, killing, and betrayal. The Bible does not sugarcoat human nature. It portrays human beings with stark realism, both individually and corporately. One is hard-pressed to find any other literature that looks at human nature and human history so realistically. The Danish philosopher Sören Kierkegaard said that when he wanted to read about human beings as we are (that is, without blinders on), he turned to the Bible and to the writings of William Shakespeare.

No one names baby boys Judas. He, after all, was the disciple of Jesus who betrayed him and later hanged himself — as scurrilous and hateful a human being as was ever born. Yet Peter, the disciple who according to Roman Catholic tradition became the first pope and after whom millions of people have named (and continue to name) their sons, betrayed Jesus not once but three times (Mark 14:66-72). Was the crime of Peter less heinous than that of Judas? At one point (Mark 8:33), Jesus even charged Peter with being Satan when he attempted to dissuade Jesus from going to Jerusalem where he would meet certain death.

So the fundamental writings of the Christian faith — the Old and New Testaments — do not pull any punches about the way we are. Why then should we be scandalized when we look at Christians, both now and in the past, acting humanly? Is it because we

17

think Christians should somehow leave their humanity behind and be closer to God than others? Or that faith should be an immunization against the follies of the human drama? Throughout history there have been those who have attempted to separate themselves from their own humanity. They have gone into the deserts to live in abject, self-imposed poverty. They have built high, thick walls to keep out the world. Some have adopted vows of silence, chastity, poverty, and obedience. Some have beaten and whipped their flesh in order to drive out thoughts and feelings that are human, all too human — such as sexual desire or the desire for revenge. Some have even believed that they succeeded in rising above the human circus. Others, from their vantage point of holiness, even thought it legitimate to persecute and kill those who failed in some way to measure up to them. One thinks of the Spanish Inquisition, which hunted down and destroyed Jews and those Christians suspected of heresy. The list of crimes against humanity, crimes committed in the name of Jesus, is a long and tragic one.

Given the treasonous and often barbaric nature of human beings, the truly perplexing thing is why God should maintain any interest in us at all. And yet, through all the treachery, through all the betrayal, through all the sheer human stupidity, God not only maintains an interest in us but loves us with a love that is beyond human comprehension. This is the central mystery that confronts us in Scripture: God could cast us off and be done with us, so why hasn't this happened? Why does God continue to love us with a love that will not let us go? God knows us better than we know ourselves. His gaze penetrates the images of piety and perfection that we hold up to him. God is not fooled for one moment. And yet ... for reasons known only to himself, God cherishes us, as the father cherished the prodigal son (Luke 15:11-32). Perhaps we will never even begin to approach an understanding of the Bible until we begin to see ourselves as characters in the story of the prodigal son — either as the one who wandered into a far country and blew his inheritance or as the righteous son who stayed home and did everything right and was horrified when the father welcomed the derelict back home.

God Has Determined Not To Be God Without Us

Theology is the attempt to comprehend God's kind of love. It is foolish to think that love can be fully comprehended. Even the love of one person for another is shrouded in a mystery that human reason cannot fully penetrate. After all, we don't *decide* to love someone. We say that we "fall in love." The whole thing is quite inexplicable. If I am pressed to explain why I love another person (that is, to give coolly analytical reasons for it), I will be brought up short and reduced to fumbling around for reasons that sound absurd as soon as I utter them. Clearly, in the matter of why love occurs at all, there is something going on that transcends reason. We can't explain it; we can only luxuriate in it and be thankful for it.

Lovers know they have the ability to irritate one another, at times beyond endurance. We parents know that, as much as we love our children, they can drive us up the wall and make us want to move away and not leave a forwarding address. Children know that parents are capable of the most stupid and, at times, hurtful things. We know very well about abusive relationships and how destructive they are. One need only consider the tragic story of Andrea Yates, the Houston mother who drowned her five children, ages six months to seven years, in the bathtub. A *Newsweek* article (July 2, 2001) describes her as a very loving person, who cared for her ailing father and neighbors who were having trouble, in addition to her own family. She was being treated for clinical depression with two antidepressant medications. Her physician had recently taken her off an anti-psychotic drug when something in this lovely woman gave way and she committed an unimaginable crime.

The nightly news is filled with stories of what goes wrong in society. Kids kill kids every day. Nations figure out new ways to pursue their own self-interests (and the consequences be damned). Apparently, it isn't just in the church that the inmates have taken over the asylum.

It might seem that in our world sweet reasonableness is the exception rather than the rule — even in the New World (North America), which was the creation of European philosophers of the eighteenth century who were passionate about reason as an antidote to the evils of history. They intended that the American experiment be exempt from the irrationality that had plagued Europe for centuries. America was to be a new beginning for the human race; hence all of the place names in America that are prefaced by the word "new": *New* England, *New* York, *New* Haven, *New* Jersey, and so on.

Nearly 500 years after the establishment of the Massachusetts Bay Colony in 1608, it seems that there is very little that is actually new about the New World. The tragic dramas of the Old World are playing themselves out on the stage of the New World all the time. Things that have plagued humanity from the beginning (war, famine, pestilence, and death — what the book of Revelation portrays as the Four Horsemen of the Apocalypse) seem alive and well, even in the New World.

And yet, as Karl Barth put it, God has willed not to be God without us. This gets at the heart of the love of God: God's unwillingness to be God without us, God's decision not to leave us behind, God's persistent need for and delight in us.[3]

"He brought me out into a broad place; he delivered me, *because he delighted in me*" (Psalm 18:19; emphasis added). We do not begin to approach an understanding of who God is until we understand him as the one who loves "the world" (John 3:16). The radical nature of this familiar verse isn't grasped until we understand that the world (*kosmos* in Greek) means "that which hates God." God so loved that which hates God (the world) that he gave his Son.

The Bible's Vital Center

The Bible is a large and bewildering book. Actually, it's a library of 66 books that came from vastly different times and settings. The question Martin Luther asked 500 years ago was this: Is there a vital center in the Bible? Is there a doctrine that, if it were removed, would destroy the Bible's story? Luther, himself a biblical scholar, discovered that there is such a vital center to the Bible. Following Saint Paul in Romans 5, he called it the doctrine of "justification by faith." This is the gospel, the good news that is really good, and apart from which the Bible would make no sense at all. Luther called this the doctrine by which the church stands or falls. Do away with this doctrine and the church and the Christian faith fall — that is, they literally die. To remove this doctrine would be similar to removing a person's heart. Death would be inevitable. The church would become just another human institution bidding for people's time, money, and attention, but with nothing to offer that is really new. It seems that we are in fact at such a point in history. Alister McGrath of Oxford University has shown conclusively that the doctrine of justification has always been regarded suspiciously by the church and has in fact usually been ignored completely.[4] Only at certain critical points has it been affirmed — for example, by Saint Augustine in the fifth century and by Martin Luther in the sixteenth.

Is this a controversial teaching? You'd better believe it! It nearly cost Luther his life. It created a rift in the Christian church that has never been healed, when Luther was excommunicated from the medieval church. It creates controversy wherever it is taught. And it is the only reason that some of us have not jumped ship and said, "Hail and farewell!" to the church. The doctrine of justification by faith is radical. It goes to the very root (Latin: *radix*) of the matter — straight to the heart.

Who would have imagined that anything having to do with the Bible and the church could be radical? It seems somehow improper. Radicals, after all, are anarchists, people who throw Molotov cocktails, who seek to overthrow the way things are. And it is precisely in this way that the gospel of justification by faith is radical. It seeks to overthrow nothing less than religion itself.

Does this confuse and unsettle you? It should. The journey we are about to embark upon is risky. It is surely controversial. It might even make you angry. I hope, however, that it will be a journey of liberation and joy.

This book is divided into five parts: 1) an introduction to the original reformer, Martin Luther; 2) the Reformation understanding of the Word of God; 3) what justification by faith means; 4) the theology of the cross; 5) the nature of the church; and 6) the re-sponsibilities of Christians for life in this world. A bibliography is included at the end of this study for those who would like to pursue matters further.

Chapter One

Martin Luther And The Beginning Of The Reformation

Luther's Early Years

Martin Luther was born in Germany in 1483, during the Age of Discovery. Eight years before Luther's birth, in 1475, Vasco de Balboa had sailed south and east from Spain and discovered the Pacific Ocean. Spain was creating an empire, looting the New World of its wealth and causing the death of indigenous populations at an alarming rate, both by the sword and by way of infectious diseases, against which the indigenous people had no defense. In 1492, nine years after Luther was born, Christopher Columbus set sail from Spain to discover a passage to India. Luther was born during the late Middle Ages, a period of Western history also known as the Renaissance (A.D. 1300-1600). He was a contemporary of the great Italian artists Michelangelo (1475-1564) and Leonardo da Vinci (1452-1519), although he probably never heard of either one.

Tradition has it that Luther was born on November 10, 1483, in Eisleben, Germany, in the province of Saxony. The next day his father took the baby to the Church of Saint Peter's in Eisleben to be baptized (many people believed that an unbaptized infant would go to hell). Because it was the Feast Day of Saint Martin, Hans named the baby Martin. Martin grew up in a large family, although little is known about the other children. The famous son overshadowed all the others. His father and mother, Hans and Margaretta, were peasants. In 1484 Hans moved his family from Eisleben, ten miles away to Mansfeld, where he worked in the copper mines and later had several men working for him. James Kittelson describes life in medieval copper mines:

Life in a copper mine in fifteenth-century Germany was far worse than working in a modern coal mine. Landslides, cave-ins, and suddenly rising water were constant, life-threatening possibilities. In addition, the miners were utterly dependent on animal power, and in particular the power of human muscle. It is no wonder that the miners had a patron saint [Saint Anne]; they needed her. Of those who survived physically, many never became more than common laborers. But Hans Luther did. Within seven years he had started his own enterprise in the copper business. Not long after that he became a member of Mansfeld's city council. Less than 25 years after Martin's birth, Hans and his partners owned at least six mineshafts and two copper smelts. Hans Luder [the way the name was spelled and pronounced at the time] was a very determined man.[5]

Martin's father attained a degree of prosperity and prominence in Mansfeld. Martin, however, was proud of his peasant roots, that he came from the common people. Although he attained a doctorate in theology and in later life liked to play the part of a Renaissance dandy, dressing in the fine attire of the day (all of which was given to him by wealthy allies) his heart remained with the German peasants. For them he translated the Bible from the original Hebrew and Greek into the German vernacular — the language spoken by people in their kitchens, work places, pubs, and on the streets.

Security was an elusive thing in the world into which Martin Luther was born. Six out of ten infants were either stillborn or died within six months. At least one of Martin's younger brothers died in infancy. Martin's mother, Margaretta, was convinced the death of the infant was the doing of the woman next door, who was suspected of being a witch. The scientific revolution was in its infancy at this time. Superstitions abounded, among the educated and the uneducated alike.

These were also the years when the plague was destroying hundreds of thousands of lives. In the city of Strasbourg, which had 25,000 inhabitants, 16,000 died in a single year. Hundreds of villages were destroyed by the plague. It would take two centuries for the land to be cultivated at its normal level of production again, because peasant farmers died in such large numbers.

It was difficult to find enough food to feed one's family on a daily basis. A drought or a wet growing season could cause the price of grain to go up as much as 150 percent over the year before. Of course there were those who made huge profits during such difficult times, but ordinary people just suffered. The number of people begging in the streets for food or who had been maimed by some accident or other or whom we would regard as mentally ill and developmentally disabled grew at an alarming rate. And those who survived more or less intact were hardened by the world in which they lived. Violence was a daily fact of life. Parents beat their children for small things, and teachers beat children who had not done their lessons adequately. "Any child caught speaking German [in Latin school] was beaten with a rod. The one who had done least well in the morning was required to wear a dunce's cap and was addressed as an ass all afternoon. Demerits were then added up for the week, and each student went home with one more caning to make the accounts balance."[6] Martin remembered being beaten with a cane fifteen times in only one morning, because he hadn't memorized his grammar lesson sufficiently.

When he was seven years old, Martin began to attend the local Latin school in Mansfeld. For seven years, he and the other boys studied how to read, write, and speak Latin. Any boy who wanted to enter one of the professions had to be proficient in it.

At age fourteen, Martin moved to a larger and better school in Magdeburg. He was away from his family for the year that he spent in the cathedral choir school there. It was run by the Brothers of the Common Life, who emphasized a warm personal faith in God and a sound knowledge of the Bible.

At age fifteen he went to his third school, which was located in Eisenach, where he studied for two years. He was happiest there, living with the family of Frau Ursula Cotta. In return for his meals, Martin looked after Frau Cotta's nephew, helped him to and from school, and tutored him. He was very fond of the headmaster of the Eisenach school, a man named Trebonius. He recalled in later

25

life how Trebonius would come into the classroom, take his hat off, and bow to the boys he was teaching. "Who knows," he would say, "which of these young students may one day be a worshipful mayor, or a doctor, or a chancellor, or even a great ruler?"

At both Magdeburg and Eisenach, Martin sang in the church choir. There were no hymns for the people to sing during the mass. The choir sang everything. His love of music was a lifelong passion. Later in life, he composed hymns and was very skilled at playing the lute, a stringed instrument similar to a guitar.

University Studies And Monastic Vows

In 1501, when Martin was seventeen years old, he began attending the University of Erfurt. There he studied Latin, logic, philosophy, geometry, arithmetic, music, and astronomy. He intended to fulfill his father's wishes and become a lawyer. A successful lawyer, married to a woman with a good dowry, would be able to support his parents in their old age. In 1505, however, all that changed dramatically. Luther became an Augustinian monk because of a close brush with death. He later recalled nearly being struck by lightning during a thunderstorm. In his terror, he promised Saint Anne, mother of the Virgin Mary and patron saint of miners, that should she spare his life he would enter the monastery. Whether the story is true or not, Martin did enter the monastery upon the completion of his master's degree at Erfurt in 1505.

Driven by an intense fear of God and anxiety about being condemned to hell at death (such fear and anxiety were common to many people of the time, because of the church's teaching that God and Christ are angry judges), Luther entered the monastery. He believed, as did everyone else, that the life of a monk would be especially pleasing to God and would gain him heaven. He entered the strictest community of his time, the Augustinian Order, which had been founded in 1243. The monastery consisted of seventy monks (sometimes also called friars), who maintained a strict discipline of prayer, study, and begging in the streets of Erfurt for money and food. The demands of the monastery appealed to Martin, because of his conviction that the harder he tried to please God by his work, study, and devotion, the better his chances would be for eternal life.

The first year of monastic life went well for him. Later he commented that the devil is always quiet during that first year. Then he began to be exceedingly troubled by his conscience. He confessed his sins over and over again, because it was taught that only a sin that had been confessed could be forgiven. He was mortified at the thought of overlooking any sin, no matter how petty or inconsequential it seemed.

In 1507 he was ordained a priest. The celebration of his first mass was a disaster, at least in his own eyes, for when it came time for him to consecrate the bread and wine (actually to change them into the body and blood of Christ, as he thought), he was mortified to be standing in the presence of the all-holy God. Roland Bainton describes the scene for us:

> Luther took his place before the altar and began to recite "We offer unto thee, the living, the true, the eternal God." He related afterward: "At these words I was utterly stupefied and terror-stricken. I thought to myself, 'With what tongue shall I address such Majesty, seeing that all men ought to tremble in the presence of even an earthly prince? Who am I, that I should lift up mine eyes or raise my hands to the divine Majesty? The angels surround him. At his nod the earth trembles. And shall I, a miserable little pygmy, say, "I want this, I ask for that"? For I am dust and ashes and full of sin and I am speaking to the living, eternal and true God.' "
>
> The terror of the holy, the horror of infinitude, smote him like a new lightning bolt, and only through a fearful restraint could he hold himself at the altar to the end.[7]

Wittenberg

In 1509 Martin was transferred from the Augustinian monastery in Erfurt to the monastery in Wittenberg. Both towns were in the province of Saxony, which was ruled by Elector Frederick the Wise. The German Empire (also at the time called the Holy Roman

Empire) consisted of 300 provinces, some of them very small, each of which was ruled by a prince. Because the princes of the seven largest provinces, elected the Holy Roman Emperor, they were called electors. Luther's prince, Frederick of Saxony, because he was one of the seven electors, wielded considerable power in the empire. Without Frederick's patronage, the Reformation might never have happened, since it was Frederick who protected Martin from those who a few years later would seek the young monk's life.

The emperor at the onset of the Reformation was Charles V, who was also king of Spain. Throughout his reign, Charles was occupied with wars with the French and the Turks. His long absences from Germany and his preoccupation with his enemies were also of great benefit to Luther and the Reformation. Charles simply didn't have time to devote to the troubles being created by a monk in Wittenberg.

The printing press had been invented by Johann Gutenberg (1390-1468) a generation before Martin Luther was born. This was also a great boon to the Reformation, because it allowed Luther's writings to be printed and distributed quickly and easily. Prior to the invention of the printing press, books were hand-lettered, a fact that made them far too expensive for the common people to own. Now books could be printed in large quantities and at a cost that made them far more accessible to a greater number of people.

There had been other attempts to reform the church prior to Luther. John Wycliffe (1330-1384) in England and Jan Hus (1372-1415) in Bohemia (the present Czech Republic) had made attempts similar to Luther's, but neither had succeeded to the same degree. Hus was burned at the stake in 1415 as a heretic, a teacher of false doctrine. A century later Martin Luther would be branded "the German Hus," a label Luther bore proudly, since he was in nearly complete sympathy with Hus. For Hus, the political and cultural situations hadn't been right for reform of the medieval church to succeed. Unlike his predecessors, Luther in 1517 enjoyed the protection of a powerful prince, the support of the German princes and the German people, the preoccupation of the emperor with other matters, and the benefit of the printing press.

Another factor that benefited Luther's reforming activities was growing German resentment against the fact that money collected by Pope Leo X in Germany was being taken out of the country to Italy, where it was being used to rebuild St. Peter's Basilica — which Germans would never see or enjoy. Pope Leo, like many other popes before him, regarded himself as an earthly monarch and surrounded himself with fine buildings and works of art. Leo's predecessor, Pope Julian, had employed Michelangelo to paint the famous frescoes on the ceiling of the Sistine Chapel between the years 1508 and 1512, just prior to the start of the Reformation.

Martin was appointed lecturer in philosophy at the University of Wittenberg, which had recently been created by Frederick the Wise. His superior at Wittenberg, Johann von Staupitz, was also a vital player in Luther's life, for it was through the friendship and love of Staupitz that young Martin began to comprehend God and the Bible in a way that was vastly different from the theology he had learned growing up.

Nevertheless, after the comparative beauties of Erfurt, Martin found Wittenberg a depressing place. In 1510, Brother Martin was appointed to travel to Rome to deal with business arising from a dispute within the Augustinian Order. This visit was eye-opening for the 27-year-old monk. He made the trip on foot over the mighty Alps. When he saw Rome, the holy city, he knelt on the ground and cried out, "Hail, Holy Rome!" But what he discovered in Rome was anything but holy. He was shocked by the way the Italian priests rushed through the mass. Luther reported hearing priests saying the words of institution so quickly that they said over the bread and wine, "Bread you are, and bread you shall remain. Wine you are, and wine you shall remain." This was supposed to be the moment of transubstantiation, when the bread and wine were literally turned into the body and blood of Christ. In turn, the Italian priests laughed at him for taking the mass too seriously. He was also shocked by the luxurious lives these priests led in the center of Christendom, by their lack of regard for their vows, and by the fact that many priests in Rome kept concubines.

It was taught by the church of the time that forgiveness of sins could be obtained by taking pilgrimages to holy places like Rome and Canterbury (Chaucer's *Canterbury Tales* depicts such a pilgrimage in fourteenth-century England) or by praying before holy relics (such as the bones of saints, remnants of the cross of Jesus, pieces of cloth from Mary's robe, drops of milk from her breasts, and so on; historians later surmised that there were enough fragments of the "true" cross of Jesus to rebuild the Spanish Armada!). And, since the time of the Crusades, a sinner could buy indulgences — official documents, purportedly signed by the pope himself, that could be purchased for the forgiveness of sins. The greater the sin, the greater the cost of the indulgence. Taking pilgrimages, praying before holy relics, and the purchase of indulgences reduced the time one had to spend in purgatory, the place of purging, which made it possible to enter heaven a pure and reborn soul. An individual could even, it was taught, reduce the time in purgatory of loved ones, who were already dead.

After climbing Pilate's Stairs on his hands and knees (the stairs Jesus had climbed in Jerusalem at the time of his trial before Pontius Pilate, which had been moved stone by stone to Rome) and saying an "Our Father" on each step — another method for reducing time in purgatory — Luther, upon reaching the top, thought to himself, "Who knows if it is really true?"

The Great Breakthrough

In 1512 Johann von Staupitz wished to retire from his position as professor of biblical theology at Wittenberg and persuaded Luther to be his successor. Martin had recently received his Doctor of Theology degree and was installed as professor of theology at the age of 28. For the next thirty years he lectured twice a week on various books of the Bible and preached nearly every day in the university chapel. His first lectures were on the Psalms. Then he went on to the New Testament books of Romans and Galatians. For his students, he had special copies of the Bible printed, which had wide margins and space between the lines so that the students could take notes as Luther lectured.

It was while preparing these lectures that the young professor made his great history-transforming discovery. He had always been frightened by the phrase "the righteousness of God," as it occurs in

Psalm 72:1 and Romans 1:17. He was not only frightened by it but had grown to hate it because, as he had been taught, it meant that God judges people for not being righteous enough. As Luther had been taught, the righteousness of God was another expression for the wrath of God. No matter how hard he had tried to measure up, he knew he couldn't. He had done all that the church required of him, and still he was terrified of God and terrified of dying. Later in his life he wrote, "I did not love, indeed I hated this just God who punished sinners."[8]

Then one day, as he was pondering these texts, he suddenly understood that the righteousness of God is not something by which God judges and condemns us but rather something that God bestows on us. Later he would call this "the happy exchange," by which Christ exchanges his righteousness for our sinfulness. Christ takes on our sin and clothes us in his holiness. The righteousness of God, Luther discovered, *is that by which God makes us righteous*. It is not at all a matter of trying harder and harder to be righteous, of going on holy pilgrimages, of praying before holy relics, or of buying indulgences. It is not even a matter of attempting to conjure up faith in ourselves — something of which we are incapable. Both faith and righteousness are gifts of God, created in us by the Spirit of God.

It was as if heaven had suddenly been opened to him:

> *It seemed to me as if I had been born again and as if I had entered paradise through newly opened doors. All at once the Bible began to speak in quite a different way to me. The very phrase "the righteousness of God," which I had hated before, was the one that now I loved the best of all. That is how that passage of Paul's became for me the gateway to paradise.*[9]

This new understanding of the Bible and of the nature of God is sometimes called Luther's great evangelical breakthrough. ("Evangelical" means "good news" or "gospel." The Lutheran church in Germany is simply called The Evangelical Church. In ancient Rome, good news from the emperor was called an "evangel." In Christian theology, the evangel is good news from God,

31

and the writers of the four New Testament Gospels — Matthew, Mark, Luke, and John — are called the four evangelists.) The word of salvation is good news, because it has nothing to do with what is expected of us. We who cannot even scratch our own backs are hardly capable of saving ourselves. If there is to be salvation at all, it must come totally from God. Martin Luther had tried the way of self-salvation, of making himself worthy to God, harder than anyone before or since, and had discovered that it simply didn't work.

Is it good works that are expected of me? he would ask. How do I know if I've done enough of them? Is it contrition for sins that is expected? How do I know if my contrition is sincere enough? Is it faith that is expected? How do I know if my faith is genuine? The best that the official theology of Luther's day could offer was that when it comes to the question of whether or not we are saved, we just have to die and hope for the best. Is that really good news? Luther didn't think so.

It was this *theological* discovery that began the movement known as the Reformation. Those who regard theology as a waste of time or as something only seminary professors are interested in often forget this. The Reformation was precisely about theology. Martin Luther was not interested in starting his own church or in becoming famous. He had no interest in or intention of breaking away from the Roman church. His greatest desire was to remain within the church, to reform it from within.

The problem, however, was that this new theological insight into the nature of the gospel would not allow that to happen. If salvation is a free gift of God, and not something I must somehow earn or buy, then the penitential system of the medieval church was completely undercut. Going on pilgrimages to holy places, the viewing of and praying before holy relics, the buying of indulgences, even the requirement that in order to be forgiven a sin has to be confessed — all of it was nullified by Luther's discovery of the righteousness of God.

This, of course, did not play well in Rome. But it played very well with the German princes and the German people, who had wearied of Rome's practice of bleeding the country financially so that the popes could live like kings.

The 95 Theses

On October 31, 1517, Martin Luther posted his famous 95 Theses on the door of the castle church in Wittenberg.[10] The church door served as the town bulletin board, where notices of all kinds were posted. This in itself was not a revolutionary act. Moreover, the theses, or statements, were written in Latin and were intended for other professors to read and debate. Within a few weeks, however, they were translated into German, printed in large quantities (thanks to the printing press), dispersed throughout the empire, and sold in every marketplace. The main point Luther was making was that God alone can forgive the punishment for sin, not the pope or his priests. The first thesis reads:

1. When our Lord and Master Jesus Christ said, "Repent," he wanted the entire life of believers to be one of penitence.[11]

This means that repentance is not a matter of indulgences, holy relics, or pilgrimages. It is not a matter of "doing penance" but of being penitent. This may at first glance appear to be a fussy, meaningless distinction, but it is at the heart of the matter and, 500 years ago, packed enough explosive power to throw all of Europe into convulsions. What did Luther mean by this distinction between doing penance and being penitent?

Two Kinds Of Relationships

First we might compare being penitent to the kind of love I have for another person: how I say her name, how I treat her in simple, everyday ways, how I long to be with her when she is gone, how I suffer when she suffers, how I look after her well-being in all things, how I cannot live in peace until a quarrel between us is resolved, and so on. H. Richard Niebuhr summed up what we mean by being in love this way:

* *rejoicing in the presence of the beloved: gratitude, reverence, and loyalty toward her*
* *longing for his presence when he is absent*

33

- *profound satisfaction over everything that makes her great and glorious*
- *wonder over his gift of companionship*
- *reverence that does not seek to absorb her or to be absorbed by her*
- *desire that she be who she is, not what he might want her to be*
- *respect for him and the profound unwillingness to violate his integrity*
- *the willingness to give my life in order to preserve hers.*[12]

In this kind of relationship my entire life reflects my love for the beloved, for this is a relationship built on profound respect and trust. All my efforts are willingly bent on caring for her, with no sense that I am obligated. Quite the contrary, I couldn't imagine not doing them. And should she die, something in me would die along with her, because this is a relationship that gives and sustains life.

This is quite different from a kind of relationship in which I do the bare minimum out of a sense of duty or obligation. This second kind of relationship is similar to what Luther meant by doing penance. It goes something like this: "Well, it's her birthday. I guess I should get her some flowers." "I tell her that I love her now and again. That should be enough to keep her satisfied." Perhaps sex happens, but it is very mechanical and quickly over — enough to satisfy "my needs." Who knows? Maybe her needs even get satisfied, but it doesn't really matter one way or the other to me. I complain about the ball-and-chain that so often describes marriage. I'd rather be out with my buddies doing guy stuff than hanging out with her and the kids.

There is a vast difference between these two types of relationships. They both claim to be relationships of love but, in the second case, I am just going through the motions out of a sense of having to keep the other happy so she'll let me have my own life apart from her. The words, "I love you," might even figure into such a relationship, but they are spoken mechanically without much investment of myself in the one whom I profess to love. Perhaps I say the words and might even accompany them with flowers now and then. And if I tire of her, I can always leave her for someone else. That's what being free means, isn't it? Think of Luther's evangelical discovery in these terms: God desires to love and be loved in the first sense. The medieval penitential system had reduced the relationship to a business transaction. As the Dominican monk Johann Tetzel, the indulgence seller in Luther's territory, crassly put it:

As soon as the coin in the coffer rings,
The soul from purgatory springs.

It's simply a matter of putting down your money and getting your reward — no contrition required. Now you've got God off your back, at least for a while, and you can resume your old self-seeking life with a clear conscience. To paraphrase W. H. Auden, "I like to sin and God likes to forgive sins. Really, the world is admirably arranged."[13]

Luther's distinction between being penitent (where your entire life reflects the love and graciousness of God, the Beloved) and doing penance (doing what you must in order to keep God off your back) is no minor thing. It is a radical distinction, one that goes to the root (*radix*) of the matter.

Forgiveness Makes Confession Possible

When forgiveness is reduced to a transaction, a business deal, it is no longer forgiveness. Forgiveness can only work its miracle between two people who care deeply enough about each other to own up to and confess their wrongdoings to each another. This is contrition and confession that matters. We can dare to own up to our wrongdoings *because* we know that the other person loves and cares about us. Were this not the case, we would forget it and simply write the relationship off.

So Luther wrote years later, in his *Large Catechism*, that God forgives us even before we think to ask for it.[14] Why would he say that? The theology of his time said that unless a sin was confessed it could not be forgiven. Confession first, then forgiveness. Luther reversed the order: forgiveness first, then confession. It is only because God issues the friendly command to confess our sins to him that we can dare to come to God in confession.

In *The Small Catechism* Luther explains the words, "Our Father who art in heaven," this way: "Here God encourages us to believe that he is truly our Father and we are his children. We, therefore, are to pray to him with complete confidence, just as children speak to their loving parents." Apart from God's command to come to him in confession, a command that carries with it the assurance that God truly loves and has already forgiven us, we would not dare come into his presence. Does this mean that we should go out and sin with abandon, since all is forgiven beforehand?

That very question betrays the fact that we still see forgiveness as a business deal of sorts. We confess and God forgives. This is love in the second sense discussed earlier: doing what we must to get by, doing what we think God expects of us so that we can get him off our backs. We confess; he forgives and leaves us alone.

When confession and forgiveness are understood in the first sense of love, the whole picture changes. Now we are talking about God the Beloved One. In a relationship of this kind, why would we want to keep doing things that will hurt the beloved? Why would we even think of forgiveness as the "freedom" to keep on hurting and destroying? It's like saying, "I like to sin and God likes to forgive sins. It doesn't get any better than that!" What place does that thinking have in a relationship in which we cherish and are cherished? Only people who are obsessed with their own warped sense of freedom as license to do whatever they want think that way. Martin Luther's evangelical breakthrough had to do with how we conceive of and relate to the source of life itself. As Saint Paul asks, "What shall we say then? Are we to continue in sin that grace may abound? By no means! How can we who died to sin still live in it?" (Romans 6:1-2).

The Church Responds To Luther

The pope and the emperor found themselves having to pay attention to an obscure Augustinian monk in the backwater town of Wittenberg. The church brought out its heavy cannons, the best scholars Europe could muster — Cardinal Cajetan of Rome and Johann Eck of the University of Leipzig — to demolish Luther. It soon became clear to Luther that he was involved in more than an academic debate between scholars. By calling the penitential system into question, Luther was challenging the power of the pope and the authority of the church itself. *A theological issue had quickly become a political one.*

Meanwhile, Martin Luther was becoming a national hero. The pope's representative in Germany wrote to Rome, "By now the whole of Germany is in full revolt; nine-tenths raise the war-cry 'Luther' while the watchword of the other tenth, who are indifferent to Luther, is 'Death to the Roman Curia [the whole structure of popes, cardinals, archbishops, bishops, and priests].' "[15] Pictures of Martin Luther, some with halos around his head, were sold in marketplaces throughout Germany. To be sure, not everyone cared about his theology. Many Germans, including some of the princes, were interested in him because he had defied the power of Rome. A number of these German backers of Luther were more interested in political independence from Rome than they were in his theology.

In May 1520 Pope Leo declared Martin Luther a heretic who could be hunted down and killed like a wild animal with the blessing of both pope and emperor. Luther had sixty days to renounce his views. On December 10, 1520, Luther gave his answer. His friend Agricola lit a bonfire near the gate of Wittenberg. "Into the flames were thrown the books of the canon law (books that set out the rules, laws, and practices of the church). Then in went books about penance that, Luther believed, had entangled the people's minds in fear. Finally, Luther himself stepped forward and threw in the papal bull *Exsurge Domine* — the document that threatened Luther excommunication, which would cut him off from the sacraments, an action that would damn Luther to hell, and which declared him a heretic, a teacher of false doctrine.[16] The papal bull flared up and burned away to ashes in the bonfire. Luther was openly defying the pope. His gesture was like a declaration of war."[17] Book burnings in our time suggest the actions of narrow-minded people who don't want others exposed to seditious ideas. In Luther's case, it was an act of defiance against a corrupt system of authority.

The Diet Of Worms

In April 1521, Luther was summoned to a gathering of electors, a diet, with Emperor Charles in the town of Worms. The church wanted the emperor to add his condemnation of Luther to the pope's, which would seal Luther's doom. The emperor had no sympathy for Luther, but he promised Luther's prince, Frederick the Wise, that Luther would have safe conduct from Wittenberg to Worms. Luther arrived on April 16, 1521, riding in a horse-drawn cart. Crowds had lined the streets of the town and cheered him on.

On April 17, Luther appeared before the emperor and was shown an enormous pile of books. He was asked whether he had in fact written them. Luther replied that he had. Then he was asked if he would reject what he had written. Luther asked for time to consider his answer. He was told very sharply that he did not deserve any more time, but the emperor granted him one day. Luther appeared once again before the emperor at 4 p.m. the next afternoon, April 18. Such a large crowd had gathered to hear his answer that the hearing had to be moved to a larger hall. By now it was getting dark and torches had to be lit. Then Luther spoke. He said that he had written three kinds of books. The first were of a devotional nature and should not be a matter of dispute. The second were books critical of abuses within the church. And some were polemical works against specific theologians. As he began to defend these writings, he was interrupted by an official of the emperor, who demanded an answer. Would he or would he not reject these writings of his?

Then Luther gave his answer, first in Latin, then in German. "Unless I am convinced, by scripture or by plain reason, I cannot and I will not recant. It is neither safe nor right to go against one's conscience. God help me. Amen."

The crowd began to shout and cheer. Luther was whisked away. A few days later he was given another chance to defend his writings, but it got nowhere. The emperor declared his verdict that Martin Luther was now to be considered an outlaw of the Holy Roman Empire and was to be excommunicated from the church. An edict was written by the emperor and posted throughout the empire. It said:

You shall refuse the aforesaid Martin Luther hospitality, lodging and bed; none shall feed and nourish him with food or drink; wherever you meet him, you shall take him prisoner and deliver him to us. As for his friends and supporters, we order that you shall attack, overthrow, seize and wrest their property from them, taking it all into your own possession. As for the books of Martin Luther, we order that nobody shall dare to buy, sell, keep, copy, print them, or support, preach, defend or assert them in any way. We decree that the works of Luther are to be burned and by this and other means utterly destroyed.[18]

The Wartburg Castle

The condemnation of church and empire hung over Luther until the day he died. It meant that he could be arrested, imprisoned, and put to death at a moment's notice — the same fate that Jan Hus had met a century earlier. Luther was "kidnapped" by friends as he journeyed back to Wittenberg. He was bundled onto a horse and taken to the Wartburg Castle for safekeeping. The kidnapping had been arranged by Frederick the Wise, who felt he could not openly defy pope and emperor. Rumors spread that Luther had been taken captive by the emperor and put to death. At the Wartburg Castle, he gave up his monk's habit and became "Knight George." He let his hair and beard grow, so that he no longer recognized himself.

Luther stayed in the Wartburg Castle a little less than a year — from April 1521 to early 1522. While he was there, he translated the New Testament from Greek to German, so that people could finally read the Bible for themselves. As James Nestingen once put it, "Luther took the Bible out of the university classroom and brought it into the kitchen." He also began translating the Old Testament from Hebrew to German but, because of the size of the task, this took several years and required help from his friends at the University of Wittenberg. He wanted to put the Bible into the simplest language possible, so that uneducated people could pray the Psalms for themselves rather than having to listen to a priest recite them in Latin, which the common people could not comprehend. Luther later used the Psalms as the basis for hymns. His well-known hymn "A Mighty Fortress" is based on Psalm 46: "God is our refuge and strength, a very present help in trouble."

Meanwhile, during Luther's absence, reforms were beginning to occur in and around Wittenberg. Monks were leaving monasteries to get married, people were being given both the wine and bread at Holy Communion (previously, they had received the bread only, for fear that they might spill the wine), and some people were eating meat on fast days. Then news reached Luther at the Wartburg Castle that mobs of his followers were breaking into churches and destroying statuary and pictures. Alarmed that such violence might easily escalate, he left the safety of the castle and returned to Wittenberg early in 1522. There he preached eight sermons against the violence that was taking place, which had been stimulated by his colleague at the University of Wittenberg, Andrew Karlstadt.

Luther wished for reform *within* the Catholic church. Never did he desire to start a church of his own. Luther's critics began to call his followers "Lutherans," a name that was intended to be derogatory. Luther's response was simple: "I ask that no one make reference to my name. Let them call themselves Christians, not Lutherans. What is Luther? After all, the teaching is not mine. Neither was I crucified for anyone."[19] He continued to wear his monk's habit, even after he had been excommunicated from the church. Moreover, to the discomfort of some present-day Lutherans, he retained a special love for the Virgin Mary. Mary has been a comfort to many Christians throughout the history of the church. After all, when it is taught that the Father and Son are both angry judges, to whom can one flee for comfort, but to the Mother? In addition, however, Mary for Luther was the model of trust in God. He wrote in a Christmas sermon:

> To this poor maiden marvelous things were announced: that she should be the mother of the All Highest, whose name should be the Son of God. He would be a King and of his Kingdom there would be no end. It took a mighty reach of faith to believe that this baby would play such a role. Well might Mary have said, "Who am I, little worm, that I should bear a King?" She might have doubted, but she shut her eyes and trusted in God.[20]

The greatest miracle, said Luther, was not that Jesus could be born of a virgin. The greatest miracle was that Mary believed the angel Gabriel's announcement that she would be the mother of Jesus.[21] It was her simple trust in what God told her that made Mary, in Luther's eyes, the model of what it means to live by faith.

Katherine von Bora

When he had returned to Wittenberg from the Wartburg Castle and heard that monks were getting married, he said, "Good heavens! They won't get *me* a wife!" At this time, Luther sought the help of Leonard Kopp, a sixty-year-old merchant in Torgau, to help nuns escape from the convent in that town. From time to time, Kopp delivered barrels of herring to the Torgau convent. On the night before Easter in 1523, Kopp bundled twelve nuns into empty herring barrels and drove them through the convent gates to freedom. Such a crime would be severely punished if discovered. Three of the nuns returned to their homes. The remaining nine went to Wittenberg. Luther felt responsible for finding them homes, husbands, or work of some kind. He was successful with eight. The ninth, Katherine von Bora, was a problem.

She had intended to marry a young man from Nuremberg who was studying at the University of Wittenberg. His family, however, objected to the marriage and it was called off. Katherine was deeply saddened by this turn of events and turned to Luther for help. He suggested a certain Dr. Glatz, but she wanted nothing to do with him. Katherine was 26 years old — practically past the marrying age. Another potential husband was turned down as well. It seems she had it in her mind that she would marry Luther himself. However, because he lived under the emperor's ban and could be arrested, imprisoned, or killed at any time, he refused even to entertain the idea of marriage. As a potential martyr, he was hardly suited for marriage. His mind was made up that he would never marry — and that was the end of the matter!

Katie and the dear Lord had something else in mind. On June 13, 1525, Martin and Katherine were betrothed. The formal marriage took place on June 27. Luther sent a wedding invitation to Leonard Kopp, which read, "I am to be married on Thursday. My lord, Katie and I invite you to send a barrel of the best Torgau beer, and if it is not good you will have to drink it all yourself."[22]

The Luthers began their marriage with no money at all. Katherine's mother had died when she was a baby. Her father had given his daughter over to the convent in Torgau to be raised. Then he remarried. He had no more interest in helping her now than he had had when she was a child. Martin had only his books and clothes. Frederick the Wise came to the rescue. He gave the Augustinian monastery in Wittenberg to the couple for their home, doubled Martin's salary as a university professor, and frequently sent wine, meat, and clothes to the Luthers.

Martin's heart was too generous. He gave away money and possessions with abandon, if it meant helping someone else. Katie, who had a much better eye for money management, had to watch him like a hawk. He had intended to give away an expensive vase to a friend as a wedding present, but, he informed his friend, Katie had hidden it.

The Luther Home In Wittenberg

The Luthers had six children: Hans, Elizabeth, Magdalena, Martin, Paul, and Margarita. Besides the eight members of the Luther family, the household was also a refuge for those needing a place to hide from the authorities, a boarding house for financially destitute students, even a hospital for the sick. And, in addition to their own children, Martin and Katie brought up four orphaned children. The household could number as many as 25 at any given time. Katie was a wife to Martin, a mother to her own children, and a nurse to those who were ill and came to her home as patients. She raised chickens and pigs and tended a huge garden to feed all the people who found their way to the Luther home. And besides all that, according to her husband she made the best beer in Germany.

Students and faculty members from the University of Wittenberg often gathered at the Luther home for meals. At such times, Martin would hold forth on a variety of topics, and the students would take notes on what he said. These notes were later collected and published as *Table Talk*. Here are recorded sayings such as these:

- *"Birds lack faith. They fly away when I enter the orchard, though I mean them no ill. Even so do we lack faith in God."*
- *"There are rumors that the world will end in 1532. I hope it won't be long. The last decade seems like a century."*
- *"What lies there are about relics! One claims to have a feather from the wing of the angel Gabriel, and the Bishop of Mainz has a flame from Moses' burning bush. And how does it happen that eighteen apostles are buried in Germany when Christ had only twelve?"*
- *"The ark of Noah was 300 ell long, 50 wide, and 30 high. If it were not in Scripture, I would not believe it. I would have died if I had been in the ark. It was dark, three times the size of my house, and full of animals."*[23]

Anfechtungen

Martin's life was in constant turmoil. He wrote endless pamphlets and books to answer charges made against him by his critics, and at times he eagerly engaged in polemics.[24] In addition, he wrote numerous commentaries on books of the Bible. His writings in German and Latin comprise 112 large volumes (published from 1883 and on as the *Weimarer Ausgabe*, Weimar Edition). And he traveled throughout Saxony in order to settle disputes among his followers. Given to periods of severe doubt and depression, he often suffered what he called attacks of *Anfechtungen*, a word that doesn't translate easily into English. "Despair" comes close, but it is more than that. It is the sense of being surrounded by evil forces, even of being abandoned by God. It was the cry of Jesus from the cross, "My God, my God, why have you forsaken me?" — a scream of desperation, the horrifying sense of being abandoned by God. When we pray in the Lord's Prayer, "And lead us not into temptation," we are asking God never to bring us to the point where we are tempted to believe that God has abandoned us.

One day Katie came into her husband's study, where she saw him so downcast that he could hardly talk. "To look at you," she

43

said, "one might think that God had died." It wasn't twentieth-century theologians who invented the notion of the death of God. Luther, 500 years ago, knew the feeling all too well. When she was fourteen, Martin and Katie's daughter Magdalena was dying. Roland Bainton describes Luther's response:

> Luther prayed, "O God, I love her so, but thy will be done." And turning to her, "Magdalenchen, my little girl, you would like to stay with your father here and you would be glad to go to your Father in heaven?" And she said, "Yes, dear father, as God wills."
>
> And Luther reproached himself because God had blessed him as no bishop had been blessed in a thousand years, and yet he could not find it in his heart to give God thanks. Katie stood off, overcome by grief; and Luther held the child in his arms as she passed on. When she was laid away, he said, "Du liebes Lenichen, you will rise and shine like the stars and the sun. How strange it is to know that she is at peace and all is well, and yet to be so sorrowful!"[25]

Old Age And Death

As he grew older Luther was frequently ill. He displayed his humanity by sometimes quarrelling bitterly with his supporters, grumbling about his students, and suffering disappointment when Wittenberg did not become the community of brotherly love he had hoped for. Early in 1546 he traveled to Eisleben, where he had been born 62 years before, to settle a local dispute. There he caught a chill and, on February 18, 1546, died. His last words were reputed to be, "We are beggars, it's true." "His friend Philip Melanchthon broke the news to the students in Wittenberg. He likened Luther to Elijah, the great prophet of the Old Testament. 'Alas,' he said, 'gone is the horseman and the chariots of Israel.' "[26] He is entombed in the Wittenberg castle church — the place where the Reformation had begun 29 years earlier when he had nailed his 95 Theses to the door on October 31, 1517.

Chapter Two

The Word Of God As Law And Gospel

The Law Kills, The Gospel Gives Life

We will never begin to understand the Bible until we are able to make the distinction between law and gospel. It is here that most interpreters of the Bible stumble, conservatives and liberals alike. Some think that the law is the Old Testament — everything that came before Christ — and that the gospel is the New Testament. But the Old Testament is filled with example after example of good news (gospel), that is, of God's graciousness toward Israel. And the New Testament has numerous passages (such as the Sermon on the Mount, Matthew 5-7) and entire books (James, for instance) that are in the form of law.

The Reformers, and especially Martin Luther, taught us to understand law and gospel very differently. You can tell the difference between law and gospel, he said, by the way the words of Scripture sound in your heart. That is to say, *the words do something to you when you hear them.* The words, "I love you," do something very different to you from the words, "Do this or face the music!"

When "I love you" is spoken, it puts a bounce in your step and might even make your heart skip a beat. These words give life and joy. Suddenly you see the sun shining and hear the birds singing. You notice the world around you in a different and lively way.

By contrast, the words, "Do this or face the music!" can create anxiety that causes your stomach to churn and boil. That's what Luther meant by hearing words with your heart. Your entire body, in fact, hears such words. The primary and most important part of interpreting Scripture is the art of distinguishing law from gospel.

Law and gospel have quite different functions, and each has a specific purpose. The law kills and the gospel gives life. Both law and gospel are of God. "The Lord kills and brings to life; he brings down to Sheol [the abode of the dead] and raises up" (1 Samuel 2:6). This is a shocking notion! God kills? How can that be? It seems so out of character for God. Isn't God supposed to love us? This is one of those points at which the Bible is very realistic about human nature. It understands better than we modern enlightened people do that there is something in us that wants to be God, that wants to be in charge, that wishes, if the truth be told, to get rid of God. This is what that ancient story about the temptation of Adam and Eve is about — the desire to be like God (Genesis 3:4). Some would call it just an ancient myth, but the truth of it is demonstrated over and over again in history.

The Fall (Uprising) Of Adam And Eve

Before the stories in the book of Genesis were written down and put into book form 3,000 years ago, they circulated among the people of ancient Israel in oral form, as stories told around campfires. Science hadn't been invented yet. It stands to reason, therefore, that there are no accounts of dinosaurs in Genesis. Ancient people knew nothing about archeological artifacts. On the face of it, the stories appear quite naive, even childlike. But those are precisely the kinds of stories people of all times and places treasure and remember — stories that tell how things came into being: the world, the sun, moon, and stars, suffering, human beings, the animals, vegetation, and all the rest of it. Such stories are called etiologies, stories that tell why things are the way they are (from the Greek *aitiologia*, "cause"). Science, which has existed as we know it for a mere 250 years, applies rigorous, rational methods in its search for the discovery of causes. The scientific method and the myriad instruments for measurement and discovery that we have (radio telescopes, the Hubble telescope, and electron microscopes) were not available to ancient peoples. Where we do scientific research, they told stories. This does not mean, however, that their stories are false. Even ancient stories are capable of illuminating truth. The stories in Genesis 1-11 tell of humanity's desire to be like God or — more accurately — to get rid of God and to become gods.

Human history, told from a completely secular point of view, confirms what the stories in Genesis tell us about human nature. We human beings seem very discontented with limits, with being finite creatures. We want it all. And it isn't good enough to point to obvious criminals of history in this regard (Nero, Hitler, Stalin, Osama Bin Laden, and all the rest), those who ruled by hate and sought power and empire for their own ideology and glorification. There is in every one of us the desire for power and control over others, a desire that seems to grow out of our own insecurities and anxieties. In order to make myself safe and secure, I need to control my environment and everyone in it. I need to know who's doing what to whom.

I need, especially, to control God or fate or whatever we might wish to call the power in the universe that seems to be beyond our control. I don't want to tempt fate by being too happy because, as the ancient Greeks taught us, when we are too happy the gods become jealous and visit all sorts of evil and suffering on us. Or I might make sacrifices in order to keep the gods off my back. That's how child sacrifice came about. A god like Molech can be placated, being the ravenous monster he is, if we throw an infant into his fiery maw every now and again. Religion has to do with keeping God or the gods or fate happy by the virtuous lives we lead and the sacrifices we make. In this way we attempt to control whatever that transcendent power is that we call God. The story of this "old-time religion" is as old as humanity itself.

"Religion": Attempting To Go Up The Down Staircase
The 1967 film *Up The Down Staircase* tells the story of a first-year teacher in a New York high school. Like a new student, she seems always to lose her way in the large, crowded building. Because there are so many students, some staircases are designated for traffic going up and others for going down. The rookie teacher, a bit scatterbrained to begin with, forgets which is which and is forever attempting to go up the down staircase. In the process, of course, she ends up going nowhere, as she is swept back down by the wave of students descending upon her.

Reformation scholar Gerhard Forde likens the usual understanding of the Christian faith to the attempt to go up the down staircase.[27] "We tend to think," Forde writes, "that faith

> *has to do primarily with 'going up' somewhere — either to heaven or to some kind of 'religious perfection.' The Christian faith is often likened to climbing a ladder or, if you like, a staircase. Take for example, the symbol of 'Jacob's ladder.' In the Middle Ages it was popular, especially among mystics, as a symbol of the struggle the Christian must undertake to reach perfection. In one way or another this kind of symbolism persists down to our own day. In my younger days, for instance, youth groups used to sing, 'We are climbing Jacob's ladder ... Every rung goes higher, higher,' with much pious fervor. And I suspect that most people still have that kind of picture in mind when they think about the Christian faith."[28]*

"Religion" is the attempt to go up the down staircase, to get from earth to heaven, to bridge the gap between ourselves and God. Its direction is upward. Religion teaches that through our good works, our piety, and our decisions for Christ, we make ourselves acceptable to God. This is how we get saved and gain heaven. Religion focuses on us. It is humanistic, because we are at the center of things. Religion teaches that in matters of salvation and damnation it is completely up to us whether we will be saved or not. Our fate, so to speak, is in our hands. The poem "Invictus," by the nineteenth-century English poet William Ernest Henley (1849-1903), sums up the spirit of religion, especially with its famous last two lines:

> *Out of the night that covers me,*
> *Black as the Pit from pole to pole,*
> *I thank whatever gods may be*
> *For my unconquerable soul.*
>
> *In the fell clutch of circumstance*
> *I have not winced nor cried aloud.*

Under the bludgeons of chance
My head is bloody, but unbowed.

Beyond this place of wrath and tears
Looms but the Horror of the shade,
And yet the menace of the years
Finds, and shall find, me unafraid.

It matters not how strait the gate,
How charged with punishments the scroll,
I am the master of my fate:
I am the captain of my soul.

Henley was a good friend of Robert Louis Stevenson, who used Henley and the sentiments expressed in this poem as the model for his character Long John Silver, the pirate, in *Treasure Island.* "Invictus" was also the source of inspiration for Timothy McVeigh, the Oklahoma City bomber. The spirit of the poem is one of defiance — defiance of the darkness, of fate ("the fell clutch of circumstance"), of the unpredictability of life ("the bludgeonings of chance"), of death ("the Horror of the shade"), of God himself (the punishments written in the scroll of the eternal bookkeeper). Henley was determined to live unafraid of it all, in the strength of his own unconquerable soul, for he was the master of his fate and the captain of his soul.

The poem found a ready and willing hearing in North America in the nineteenth century. Its lines worked themselves into the American collective unconscious so that it continues to find a hearing, even at the present time (think of Frank Sinatra's song, "I Did It My Way"). It expresses our sense of independence, of making it on our own strength and by our own lights, without help from anyone else — including God, if need be. We have plotted our course and we will forge ahead, in spite of our own misgivings, our fears, or anything else that gets in our way. There is something noble about this swashbuckling approach to life.

Yet one need only look at the fate of the indigenous populations in the New World to see how this self-directed, devil-may-care spirit has actually worked itself out.[29] Nothing and no one was allowed to deflect our forebears from the task of subduing this continent and bending its rich resources to their will. It only remains for us, their descendents, to question what frontiers we should conquer next. Outer space appears to be our frontier, even though it seems a bit arrogant to think of "conquering" such vastness. In a former time, the drive to conquer was understood as a matter of "manifest destiny." It appeared to be manifest (self-evident) that God had delivered the world into the hands of Americans. It was our divinely mandated destiny to civilize the savage world, to bring the world under our control. This is the nature of empire. Empires seek to control other peoples and nations, not only for economic purposes, but for security purposes as well. The wider the net of empire is cast, the more secure those within the empire feel. This worked while the Roman army was invincible. The time came, however, when even that army could not keep the barbarians outside the gate. The Roman Empire did not fall all at once. It took many years.

The attacks on the World Trade Center and the Pentagon on September 11, 2001, were attacks on the symbols of the American Empire — our financial power and our military power. Following the attack, the *Los Angeles Times* reported that the sale of Bibles, self-help books, and gas masks skyrocketed. Suddenly a deep anxiety has pervaded American life. We are no longer immune to the ravages of war, no longer protected by two vast oceans from the rest of the world. And we wonder whether we ever will return to "normal" again — life as we once knew it. The answer is that those days are over. Will we learn what it means to live by faith, by trust in the promises of God, or will we become increasingly desperate in our attempts to secure ourselves from the enemy?

Religion has to do with power and control. It was born in the story of the building of the Tower of Babel (Genesis 11), which was in effect a coup d'état, a revolt against God. It is said that God helps those who help themselves, but God's track record isn't a very good one. Look at all of the undeserved suffering that goes on in the world. God doesn't seem particularly adept at feeding the millions who starve to death in the world every year. Nor does God seem particularly to care that millions die — most of them children. God most likely won't place three meals a day on my table if I don't earn the money to buy groceries. Having anything in this world requires that I work for it, that I go out and get it. And if I work hard enough and am diligent, I will attain the great American dream and be "fulfilled."

The same logic seems to apply also to heaven. If I want heaven, I need to go get it. We need to do it the old-fashioned way, as the investment firm Smith-Barney says: "We EARN it!" Build a tower and besiege the citadel of God, if need be. Or, if my disposition is not suited to taking heaven by storm, I need at least to make the effort to prove myself worthy of it by living an exemplary life. Or, at the absolute minimum, I need to accept Jesus Christ as my personal Lord and Savior. I've got to do *something!* There is after all no free lunch. It must be earned — somehow or other.

This is the message of "religion." Whether you go to heaven or hell is up to you. God sits on the sidelines of the drama of life (or above it all in heaven) and watches to see what you are going to decide and how you are going to make yourself worthy of God's love. You are the active one; God is passive. You are at the center of the drama; God is outside of it or above it. You are in charge of what happens; God is at your beck and call, for God helps only those who help themselves. Religion, in short, is humanistic, because we human beings are at the center of things. It is we who determine what will happen to us.

The Nature Of Christianity

But isn't Christianity also a religion? No, it is not. Christianity reverses everything that religion stands for, tips it upside down. If religion is human-centered (anthropocentric), Christianity is God-centered (theocentric). If the message of religion is, "It's all up to you," the message of Christianity is, "It's all up to God." God is the giver; we are the receivers. If in religion we are active and God is passive, in Christianity God is active and we are passive. If religion teaches us that we have to "go up the down staircase," the message of Christianity is that God has come *down* to us, in the babe born in the manger.

51

The problem with religion, as Martin Luther discovered 500 years ago, is that you can never be sure that you've done enough to satisfy God. Perhaps your faith isn't pure enough. Maybe your decision for Christ wasn't sincere enough. Suppose you haven't done enough good works? How do you know if and when God is satisfied with the things you do? Is salvation a game of chance in which you do your best and hope it's good enough?

The focus in such thought is on you. And the questions such a focus raises are relentless and endlessly anxiety producing. Have *you* done enough? Is *your* faith strong enough? Was *your* decision for Christ sincere? Are *you* sure?

Martin Luther tried all of that 500 years ago. He prayed more than was required of the monks in his monastery. He inflicted punishment upon himself with a whip, to the point of passing out. He deprived himself of sleep. He begged for food on behalf of the hungry. Yet no amount or penance, prayer, and good works put his heart and mind to rest regarding God. He was haunted by the fear that perhaps it wasn't enough. Perhaps it would never be enough.

Does this go absolutely against everything you have ever believed and been taught? Is it a bit frightening? For if the message of Christianity is right, then all of the power and control belongs to God and we are quite literally not in control. Our fate rests in the hands of God, whom we have never seen. We might suspect that God is out there somewhere, but we can't be sure that he is for us (*pro nobis*). To look at the sorry state of the world, we might suspect that God is against us (*contra nobis*). We might even suspect that God is not there at all, that we are on our own in an overwhelmingly large universe, that it doesn't matter whether we are here or not. The thought may even haunt us that it isn't at all clear whether there is a purpose to life, a purpose or meaning that goes beyond being born, making a living, and dying. If there is such a purpose, it doesn't always seem apparent. In that case, it may be best to follow the logic of "Invictus": Damn the torpedoes, full speed ahead. Whatever happens, happens.

There is a certain sense of liberation in that approach to life. We do the best we can with the hand we've been dealt, work hard, keep our noses to the grindstone, keep them relatively clean, pay our bills, have some fun along the way, and not worry about questions of meaning, questions of purpose, and especially not about questions pertaining to God. Whatever happens to us when we die, happens. We'll worry about it then — if ever.

Faith

But we don't need to live like that. A child forever wondering if she is loved and cherished by her parents would know nothing of security, because she would have no rock-bottom certainty that, no matter what happens, she will always be deeply cherished. She would always wonder, "How do they really feel about me?" And she would spend her days doing everything to keep them happy with her. At some point, out of disgust she might simply write her parents off. "Why waste time and energy worrying about what they think of me? I'll just do the best I can to make it on my own." And the sad thing is that a lot of kids grow up that way — literally on their own.

Faith is the complete opposite of this terrible uncertainty. A child who knows that she is well loved by her parents and who is not haunted by wondering how her parents really feel about her has the confidence to enter life, to take risks, even to fail, without being devastated by the experience. She has a solid foundation on which to stand, even when the ground beneath her shakes and rolls. She knows where home is, even when she's far away. Simply put, she trusts her parents — she has faith in them.

This faith or trust in her parents is not something she drummed up in herself. She didn't one day decide they were probably trustworthy and say to them, "I've decided to accept you as my parents." What nonsense that would be! On the contrary, her parents created this trust in her by demonstrating day after day in ways both large and small that they indeed love her and will never forsake her. This had been going on long before she was even born. Even before her mom was pregnant with her, her parents wondered what their children would be like. Would they be boys or girls? Who would they look like? What would they be interested in? The baby was loved and cherished long before she saw the light of day. She was born into a family who would surround her and nurture her. How silly it would be to talk about "deciding" to accept such love and nurture. It was all there a long time before she was even conscious of it. She couldn't have survived without it. Sad to say, this sort of thing isn't experienced by every child. Some are unwanted or treated to doses of alcohol and crack cocaine and are born already addicted. Others are brutalized by parents or other adults and never know what it means to be loved. As they grow up, they may never know how to love in return. They will never know what it means to trust another person, to be surrounded by the nurturing cocoon called family. But this is not God's desire for us.

Faith is trust, whether it is trust in another person or in God. If I say I believe in you, it means I trust you. To have faith in God is infinitely more than to believe that God exists. Besides, there is no way to prove or disprove the existence of God. Arguments for the existence of God (such as Thomas Aquinas's five proofs) end by talking about empty abstractions like an Unmoved Mover or a First Cause — something or someone who set the universe in motion. These arguments, however, really say nothing whatsoever about the *character* of this god. The Unmoved Mover could very well be evil. There's enough evidence in the world to lead one to conclude that whoever or whatever created the universe may be evil rather than good.

Martin Luther wrote in his *Large Catechism* that that to which we look for all good and flee for refuge is God.[30] What Luther means is that anything or anyone can become God for us. Whatever or whomever we fear, love, and trust above all else is God for us. It can be fame, fortune, the stock market, a political leader, success, a car, even yourself — anything or anyone at all. We know that life in this world is very fragile and that events are all too often out of our control. Life, family, work, home, health, a sense of meaning — any or all of it can be taken from us in the blink of an eye. Yet we can't live without trusting. Getting out of bed in the morning is an act of faith. We get up without knowing for certain what the day holds — either for good or ill. Some days we wish we had stayed in bed. Going to sleep is an act of faith, for when we are asleep, we are totally defenseless. Moreover, we go to sleep not knowing whether we will even wake up.

Living requires that we place our trust somewhere. We who live in the modern world, especially those of us who live in North America, have been taught to be self-sufficient and self-reliant. These are good and noble attributes. Self-sufficiency and self-reliance transformed the North American wilderness into a thriving civilization (albeit at the expense of those who called the wilderness home). These noble attributes, however, have a dark side to them. Self-sufficiency and self-reliance, the characteristic attributes of rugged individuals, have left us isolated and disconnected. These attributes provide no basis whatsoever for community — not even for the most basic of communities, the family.

The question is whether there is anything or anyone we can trust completely and unconditionally with our very lives. The answer of Scripture is that, in and of ourselves, we are absolutely incapable of such trust. Without fail, time and again we will place our ultimate trust in something or someone that is less than ultimate. We are apparently incapable of doing otherwise. As John Calvin (1509-1564), Luther's younger contemporary at Geneva, understood so well, the human mind and heart are idol factories. An idol demands ultimate trust, but is not itself ultimate. An idol, to put it differently, is something finite that claims to be infinite.

Scripture teaches that God alone can create faith in us. With only the aid of our own lights, we seem either to conclude that there is nothing ultimate in the universe, or that God is out there somewhere, but we can never be quite certain what he's up to. So how does God create faith in us? The answer lies in the nature of the Word of God as law and gospel.

Back To Law And Gospel
The law has two functions, a civil function and a theological function. The civil function is to keep order in society, to protect life. Without laws to govern how we go about conducting our daily life there would be anarchy. No one would be safe; life would not be protected; and nothing could get done. Even with laws in place there can be disorder. Imagine what it would be like if there were

55

no laws to constrain us at all. The law operates in society to keep a lid on things, to make life together possible in spite of all the differences that exist among us.

Second, the law has a theological function or use. Here the law is the voice that accuses us of not measuring up. The Reformers stated it this way: *Lex semper accusat*, the law always accuses. It is that voice that comes in the middle of the night when the household is quiet, the voice that eats away at you by reminding you of your failures and of your inadequacies as a person. The voice of the law is unrelenting. It is what literally drives some to drink. Alcohol is able, at least for a while, to dull the accusing voice.

But the law attacks in other ways as well. It does so by reminding us in any number of ways that we are going to die. The day will come when the Grim Reaper will appear at your door. The law attacks by reminding us that all roads lead to the cemetery. And the fact that we will die might mean that nothing in this life is worthwhile. Nothing we achieve will last forever. We will be forgotten, even if a town or street or baseball stadium is named after us. After a while, the name of the town will just be a name. No one will remember the person who went with it.

And the law attacks by holding up the wrath and judgment of God before our eyes. Perhaps I can't bring myself to believe there is a God. All that God-talk seems too strange, too unscientific, too incredible. And yet, when the reality of death comes home to me, I might worry, just a little, that I will be forced to meet some sort of God — and I will have to do it alone. What will happen to me then?

The law also attacks by showing me how unfulfilled I really am. Life in America is supposed to be fulfilling. We assume that fulfillment is our right. If we work hard, we're entitled to a life free from want. But when I look at how it has actually gone, sometimes my life seems strangely lacking. Perhaps I should have worked in some other profession, or gone to college, or not wasted my time in college, or tried harder to be a better parent to my children. If only I hadn't made such bad investments, we would have more to live on now. If only I had taken my mother's advice and married Paul instead of Harry, I would have been happier.

The past sits back there with its broken dreams, bad choices, and failures and mocks us. We can't do anything about the past, so why does it always come back to haunt us with questions and regrets that won't go away.

These are all manifestations of the law — the voice that accuses us of not measuring up, of falling short, of being deficient. Sometimes it hits us hard. At other times it eats away at us subtly and quietly. But it always does its work of cutting the ground out from beneath our feet and raising our anxiety and blood pressure levels. In this way, the law kills us. It backs us into a corner and provides no means of escape. We find ourselves trapped by what Scripture calls "the wrath of God."

Luther called the accusing work of the law God's alien or strange work (Isaiah 28:21).[31] This is the work of the hidden God (Isaiah 45:15).[32] In North America we are not accustomed to hearing about things like the hiddenness of God or the alien work of God. God has always seemed to us to be much more straightforward. If we do what God expects of us, we say, then we are entitled to expect good things of God. If we don't live up to God's expectations, we can expect the worst. It's as simple as that. At least it ought to be as simple as that, because we have other things to do. Besides, we don't go in much for complications — especially when it comes to religion. We do our bit, God does his bit, and that's that. What more do you want?

The problem is that we aren't that simple and straightforward and neither is our experience of the world. We lead moral and upright lives (at least most of the time). We do what the boss, the nation, and the church expect of us. We work hard and keep our noses clean. We don't intentionally break the law (well, we may drive too fast now and then and run a stop sign when no one's looking). We don't go out of our way to break the Ten Commandments. On the whole, we should get a passing grade from God when we die — maybe not an A+, but at least a C or a B. What more can anyone, including the Man Upstairs, ask? The prospect of being audited by the Internal Revenue Service is probably more frightening to us than the prospect of being judged by God. Besides, the judgment of God should be reserved for those notorious criminals who spend their lives harassing and brutalizing others. This kind of reasoning on the part of good, upright, law-abiding citizens seems irrefutable. I've done what's been expected of me; now give me my reward.

Notice, however, what has happened. Once again, our relationship to God has been reduced to the level of a business transaction. A relationship that was intended as one of love has been reduced to the level of a bargain. Good behavior is rewarded. Bad behavior is punished. That isn't a relationship in which those who are involved are cherished. It's more like a treaty between hostile nations, in which we agree not to destroy each other — at least not entirely.

The strange, alien, hidden work of God is to smash and destroy that sort of thing. Luther often described the law of God as "a hammer or an anvil that smashed down human pride and made room for God's love."[33] Without this alien work of God, there is no room for love. We merely do what is expected of us, in order to use God to get what we want — life in the Big Rock Candy Mountains.[34]

Luther compared us to drunken peasants attempting to ride horseback. It's very difficult to ride when you're drunk. You sway from side to side, as the horse moves and end up falling off on one side or the other. Either you fall off on the side of arrogance, or you tumble off on the side of despair.

The voice of arrogance says, "Whatever God requires, I can do by myself. I don't need God's help or anyone else's, for that matter." The voice of despair says, "I will never measure up. There's no hope for me."

On the one hand, we might become so impressed by our own goodness, virtue, righteousness, and faith that we don't even recognize how far we have moved away from the relationships that make for life (relationships with other people, with the good earth, with the very Source of life). Or, on the other hand, we might lose hope entirely and take no pleasure in life, the people around us, our daily work, or the Father in heaven. Luther knew this state of being very well. He had tried the first option — doing what God and the church expected of him. He tried with all his might, but always went from arrogance to despair. (When he was low Luther would seek out company, even the company of his and Katie's pigs.)[35] He knew from his own experience that despair is closer to faith than we might at first think, since faith in God begins when we learn to despair of our own virtue and righteousness. Moreover, very often our arrogance is simply a cover for our despair — the brave, determined face we show God and the world, all the while drying up within, like a flower that has been plucked from the life-giving soil, and assuming that's the way life is supposed to be.

The law exposes arrogance and despair for what they are: the absence of trust. Without trust, which is another word for faith, life shrivels up and dies. One can continue to draw breath, eat three meals a day, and go to work, but such "life" is spiritless. The law holds up a mirror for us to look in and says, "See how lifeless you are." The law cannot save us. Keeping the Ten Commandments perfectly cannot save us. The law is not a ladder to heaven that we can climb. The law always and only accuses us of falling miserably short of what we were intended to be. It says, "This is what you were meant to be, but look how you've failed to measure up. You aren't as loving as you should be. You aren't as fulfilled as you should be." And the law prods us to *try harder!* Like a National Football League coach in preseason training camp or a drill sergeant in boot camp or a boss who won't give us a break or the voice of perfectionism that lives in some of us, the law pushes and cajoles and mocks us for not measuring up, until it finally beats us down completely.

The law functions in its theological sense as a goad or whip to drive us further and further away from God. It literally turns our face towards hell until we flee to Christ for mercy. Then the law (God's strange or alien work) has accomplished its purpose. It has shown us that we do not have life in ourselves. It has demonstrated that our best efforts to fulfill ourselves, to save ourselves, and to find that elusive happiness we hear so much about amounts to nothing. It has shown that religion is bankrupt. It has opened our ears, so that we can finally hear the gospel, the word that gives life.

The gospel is simply this: You are loved by the Creator and Sustainer of the universe not because you deserve such love but only because God has decided to love you. Who deserves to be loved by another? Love is the miracle that happens *in spite of* everything that militates and argues against it. As we hear of the love God has for us, little by little our suspicions of God are worn down and our favorite idols are reduced to rubble. God is the lover who (to use a word from an earlier generation) woos us, who will not leave us alone until our love has been won. This is what it means to say that God is a jealous God. He will not allow anything to come between you and him — not even your distrust or hatred of him. No barriers are too great for God to overcome — not even our rejection of God. This God, as Karl Barth says, does not will to be God *without us*. "You did not choose me," Jesus says, "but I chose you" (John 15:16). It's exactly like the parents, who refuse to let their child go through life alone. Such a thing would be unthinkable for earthly parents, and it is just as unthinkable for God.

The law (God doing his strange work) smashes our idols, our misconceptions, and every other barrier that seeks to separate us from him, so that the gospel can finally be heard: God's "I love you."

Chapter Three

Justification By Faith

"Uncertainty is the most miserable thing in the world."
— Martin Luther, *The Bondage of the Will*

Justification: A Doctrine That
Never Made It To North America

Justification by faith is the heart of Scripture. To remove this teaching would be to remove that which makes the Old and New Testaments unique. Apart from the doctrine of justification, the Bible would be a book of laws. There simply would be no gospel, no good news.

Saint Paul states it this way, "For by grace you have been saved through faith, and this is not your own doing; it is the gift of God — not the result of works, so that no one may boast" (Ephesians 2:8-9). We are saved by faith, says Paul, and this is not our own doing. Faith or trust in God is the creation of God, God's gift of grace; therefore, we have nothing to boast about, because we had nothing to do with it. *Articulus stantis et cadentis ecclesiae* (on this article the church stands or falls).

Sadly, this teaching is little known in North America. In 1939 German theologian Dietrich Bonhoeffer (who was martyred by the Nazis on April 9, 1945) made a report to his German colleagues after having studied at Union Theological Seminary in New York City. The report is titled "Protestantism without Reformation." Bonhoeffer reported that he did not encounter Reformation teachings in America. Moreover, when he spoke of justification by faith, Americans seemed to think he was speaking a foreign language. The biblical teachings that the Reformers had rediscovered, through great struggle and at the risk of losing their lives, never found their way to the New World.

What did find their way to America were 1) the humanism of Erasmus of Rotterdam (1466-1536), Luther's older contemporary in the Netherlands, which emphasizes moral behavior and our freedom to accept or to reject God's grace, and 2) the social and moral teachings of John Calvin (1509-1564), Luther's younger contemporary, which emphasize the Christian's duty to transform secular society. Calvin shared Luther's stress on justification by faith, but that part of Calvin's theology never made it across the Atlantic either.

What Does It Mean To Be Justified?

The word "justification" is taken from the ancient law courts. Someone accused of a crime is brought before the judge. The evidence is heard and the judge has the power to declare the accused either guilty or not guilty. If the verdict is "not guilty," the accused is set free and is said to be "justified."

Oddly enough, however, when Saint Paul writes of justification in the sight of God, it is precisely the guilty who are declared righteous — that is, who are justified. It was while we were sinners, enemies of God, that Christ died for — the godly? No, for the ungodly (Romans 5:6-11). This puts a completely different twist on it. We are declared righteous, innocent, and just — even though we are as guilty as sin.

Here there is no quid pro quo, no "If you will only straighten up and fly right, then God will love you." That whole "if ... then" way of thinking is simply blown out of the water. Whenever the word "if" shows up in talk of God's relationship with us (for example, "*If* you have faith, then God will love you"; "God's grace is effective *if* we accept it"; "*If* you do your part, God will do his"), we can be certain that such talk is not good news. It is law, not gospel. Unfortunately, the law is very often proclaimed as though it were the gospel.

It's like saying to someone, "I will love you *if* you fulfill certain requirements. If you fail to live up to any of them, however, the deal will be off." Can such talk really be said to be about love? Of course, analogies always break down at some point. For a variety of reasons, human relationships do end. But justification is qualitatively different from any human relationship. This relationship will not end for any reason, for we are dealing with the God who does not will to be God *without us*. Even when we fall away from God, he never abandons us, but pursues us like the lover he is.

The God who justifies the ungodly is portrayed beautifully in Psalm 139. Here is described the God who would later be praised by Saint Paul in Romans — the God who knows us better than we know ourselves and from whom absolutely nothing about us is hidden. Before we sit down or stand up, he knows about it. He discerns our thoughts before we even have them. If we seek escape from his presence, we cannot hide from him — not even if we make our beds in Sheol, the abode of the dead. Even darkness cannot hide us from him, for darkness is as light to him.

A Love That Subverts Our Entire Experience

British poet Francis Thompson knew this God well and described him in a poem titled "The Hound of Heaven." Francis Thompson was born in 1859 to a respectable Catholic family. His father, a physician, sent Francis to Ushaw College (a Catholic college in the north of England dedicated to training priests) in the hope that his son would become a priest. This did not happen. The eighteen-year-old Francis was sent back home by the headmaster of the college with a letter that Francis was not cut out for the priesthood. For the next six years, Francis led a rather haphazard life. He studied medicine, but failed the medical examinations three times. Sometime during the six years, he became addicted to opium, which was readily available in England in the form of laudanum and which doctors prescribed as a painkiller and sedative. Factory workers spent their week's pay on it; and mothers quieted their fretful babies with it. After failing his medical examinations for the third time, Francis became an addict.

In the winter of 1887, Wilfrid Meynell, editor of a Catholic literary magazine called *Merry England*, received a parcel containing an essay and some poems. The parcel also contained this letter:

Dear Sir,

In enclosing the accompanying article for your inspection, I must ask pardon for the soiled state of the manuscript. It is due, not to slovenliness, but to the strange places and circumstances under which it has been written. I enclose a stamped envelope for a reply. [I will regard] your judgement of its worthlessness as quite final. Apologizing very sincerely for my intrusion on your valuable time, I remain,

Yours with little hope,
Francis Thompson

Kindly address your rejection to the Charing Cross Post Office.[36]

Meynell put the parcel in his desk, where it remained for the next three months. When he did finally read the material, Meynell wanted to publish it but was unable to reach the young poet. In the April issue of the journal, Meynell published one of the poems. Shortly thereafter, Francis Thompson showed up in the editor's office strung out on opium. Meynell and his wife, Alice, took charge of the young man, sending him to a clinic to dry out and then to a monastery to recover.

Thompson wrote most of his poetry during the ensuing four-year period of sobriety. The most widely read of them was "The Hound of Heaven," which is based on the Psalm 139. By 1898, Thompson had resumed using opium and died nine years later, in 1907, from tuberculosis and laudanum poisoning.[37] It is obvious that Francis Thompson suffered from clinical depression and used laudanum to alter his depressive moods.

"The Hound of Heaven" is a lengthy poem, 182 lines long — too long to quote here in its entirety. It begins, however, this way:

I fled Him,[38] down the nights and down the days;
I fled Him, down the arches of the years;
I fled Him, down the labyrinthine ways
Of my own mind; and in the mist of tears
I hid from Him, and under running laughter.
Up vistaed hopes [hopes seen at a distance] *I sped;*

And shot, precipitated,
Adown Titanic glooms of chasmed fears,
From those strong Feet that followed, followed after.

The poet found himself hounded by One, he thought, who would surely destroy him, so utterly relentless was the pursuit. At the end of the poem, the Pursuer says:

And human love needs human meriting:
How hast thou merited —
Of all man's clotted clay the dingiest clot?
Alack, thou knowest not
How little worthy of any love thou art!
Whom wilt thou find to love ignoble thee,
Save Me, save only Me?
All which I took from thee I did but take,
Not for thy harms,
But just that thou might'st seek it in My arms.
All which thy child's mistake
Fancies as lost, I have stored for thee at home:
Rise, clasp My hand, and come!
Halts by me that footfall:
Is my gloom, after all,
Shade of His hand, outstretched caressingly?
"Ah, fondest [most foolish], *blindest, weakest,*
I am He Whom thou seekest!
Thou dravest [drives] *love from thee, who dravest Me."*

This is a great love story. Francis Thompson discovers at last that to be loved by another human being requires some beauty or meritorious quality in the beloved, but that with God it is infinitely different. "Whom wilt thou find to love ignoble thee, save Me, save only Me?" Here is a love that wondrously subverts the poet's entire experience — and our own as well.[39]

This is precisely what justification by faith is about. God will not rest until we fear, love, and trust him above all else (the phrase is from Luther's *Small Catechism*) until we live by faith in him alone. That is to say, God will not rest until he has recreated us. If now we flee from him, whether motivated by fright (as with Francis

Thompson), by doubt (as with Saint Augustine), or by hatred of God (as with Luther), the Beloved will not cease his search for us until he has restored us as his beloved daughters and sons.

Martin Luther knew that birds, dogs, and babies sense this, while the rest of us struggle mightily with it, thinking we somehow have to deserve or merit or be worthy of the love in which birds, dogs, and babies simply luxuriate.

Luther also knew the terrible sense of uncertainty that comes from not knowing whether salvation is yours. There is nothing worse than that kind of uncertainty, being told that you have to wait until you die to see whether God will save you. To approach death with that kind of uncertainty would be frightening indeed. It would be like growing up and never being quite sure what your parents thought of you.

The doctrine of justification is the pledge God makes to us that he does indeed love us. Saint Paul speaks of Christ as the One who "will also strengthen you to the end, so that you may be blameless on the day of our Lord Jesus Christ [the day Christ returns]. God is faithful; by him you were called into the fellowship of his Son, Jesus Christ our Lord" (1 Corinthians 1:8-9). Justification is about the faithfulness of God, who remains faithful to us even when we are unfaithful to him (Romans 3:5-11). This is the kind of love a true parent has for his or her children. If we as earthly parents know how to love this way, why should we imagine God is any different?

But God does not leave it here. To drive home the fact of his love for us, to help us grasp it, he gave us the sacraments: Baptism and Holy Communion. Most Reformation churches celebrate two sacraments, the two that were instituted by Jesus himself in the New Testament. Both sacraments use common earthly elements: water in Baptism, and bread and wine in Holy Communion. These elements, combined with the promise of Christ to be present in them, create a sacrament. How is Christ present in the water, bread, and wine? We can't really say. All we know is that he has promised to be there, to meet us at the baptismal font and the communion rail. And, like Mary, we simply take God at his word!

The message of justification is brought home in these sacraments. God wasn't satisfied just to pronounce us "not guilty" or merely to say, "I love you." God wanted the words to take on substance so that we can actually see, feel, taste, and touch his love for us. Water is poured over the baby's or adult's head. The sound and feel of the water, the fact that the pastor and the baptized get wet — these are physical signs of God's love for this person.

When you drink the wine and chew on the bread, you are actually feeling and tasting the love of God for you. There is no mistaking the pungent taste of the wine as it slides down your throat. It's something you have to pay attention to. It may even cause you to cough and make your eyes water. The bread may stick stubbornly to the roof of your mouth. The dear Lord wants you not only to hear his declaration of love for you but to experience it with all your senses. This is so, simply because we often refuse to hear. God thereby makes his declaration of love visible, tangible, and unmistakable.

The problem, of course, lies with us. We can't believe that we are loved. Perhaps we can't even believe that another human being could love us. "If she really knew what I was like," we think to ourselves, "she would leave me in a second." "If he knew my deepest secrets, he wouldn't want me." Therefore, even between us human beings, we need to say the words "I love you" over and over again, until they finally start to sink in and we begin, however hesitantly, to believe that it's true.

This is how hearing creates love and faith. "So faith comes from what is heard, and what is heard comes through the word of Christ" (Romans 10:17). We cannot possibly summon up faith in ourselves, especially not faith in God, whom we can't even see. Faith must come from God, who, like a persistent lover, keeps telling us over and over again, "I love you, I love you." When we read it in the Bible and hear it from the preacher and feel it in water, bread, and wine, sooner or later, by the grace of God, it begins to sink in — and faith — that is, trust — in God begins.

God doesn't tell us to go out and find faith somewhere, and then (and only then) he will love us. Rather, he woos us and wins us over, like the lover he is. When faith is born, when we actually

67

begin to trust God and to live as beloved children, God is satisfied. God will not be satisfied until this happens. And God will use all means at his disposal, even the terrible threat of his wrath, if it will cause us to run for cover to Christ. That's the point of the three parables in Luke 15: the lost sheep, the lost coin, and the lost son (otherwise known as the prodigal son). God will not rest until he has searched us out and found us.

Part of our problem is that so much that passes for Christian faith is utterly despicable. The very words *God, Christ, Bible, church* and the many others that are bound up in the vocabulary of faith may make us sick to our stomachs or make us fighting mad because of the way these words have been abused, or because of the many ways, small and large, that we have been hurt by religious people. One medieval wag put it this way, "I would rather see coming at me a thousand Turks armed with swords and spears than one lone Christian who is convinced that he is doing the will of God."

Unfortunately and tragically, Christians have been the worst enemies of Christ, as we have used the Bible and the vocabulary of faith to bludgeon people, to make them conform, and to beat them into submission. There are Christians and there are churches that are simply obnoxious and stupid. There are pastors who spend their entire lives in search of something intelligent to say, and fail.

And then there are those towering figures, so often forgotten, especially in the North American context (because we don't like history): Saint Augustine (fourth century), Martin Luther and John Calvin (sixteenth century), Jonathan Edwards (eighteenth century), Sören Kierkegaard (nineteenth century), and the giants of the twentieth century — Karl Barth, Paul Tillich, Rudolf Bultmann, Dietrich Bonhoeffer, Reinhold Niebuhr, H. Richard Niebuhr, and a host of others throughout the past 2,000 years, who were intelligent and compassionate Christians of integrity. These people can help us get past the distortions, stupidity, and destructiveness of what often passes for Christian faith. Standing on their shoulders allows us to see beyond the distortions, to rediscover the Bible and the great tradition of Christian theology — perhaps for the first time — and to discover there the beauty and wonder of this One who loves us beyond any earthly comparison. This is the beginning of liberation and joy.

Chapter Four

The Theology Of The Cross

"A theologian of glory calls evil good and good evil.
A theologian of the cross calls the thing what it actually is."
— Martin Luther, *Heidelberg Disputation of 1518*

The Lure Of Illusions

No human being can absorb the full onslaught of experience.
For one thing, there is simply too much of it. To know about everything would be an unendurable curse. No suffering, no matter how
small, would escape our notice. It is difficult enough in the contemporary world that we have print and electronic media bringing
the world into our consciousness every day. Perhaps we know more
than is good for any of us. The danger of being aware of too much
is that we can easily become overwhelmed by what goes on within
and around us. The temptation, then, is to jump to the conclusion
that nothing that we could possibly do would make any difference
in the world. It will, we cynically assume, go on its way with or
without us. In short, we resign ourselves to the power of fate.

The human ego is equipped with a system of defense mecha-
nisms whose purpose is to protect the fragile ego from exposure to
too much reality. One of these defenses is denial. When we hear of
the death of someone dear to us, our first response is to deny that
the report is true. "I just talked with her this morning. How could
she be dead a few hours later?" "The doctor says I have incurable
cancer, but it can't be true. After all, I've always taken care of
myself." Denial operates like the numbness that occurs when we
physically injure ourselves. The injury sets in motion the production of endorphins, which are the body's naturally produced mor-
phine. The numbness allows us to ignore the wound long enough
to seek help. But grief is sneaky and can take us by surprise when

our defenses are down. Something remembered — the smell of burning leaves, something someone says, a dream — any of these things and a host of others can trigger the painful memory and send us reeling into grief.

If we are to go on living we must at some point deal with tragedy. Often this requires the help and support of others. Contrary to popular wisdom, time does not necessarily heal all wounds. The simple passage of time isn't enough, because we are equipped with memory and emotion. To memory, time does not exist. The act of remembering transports us right back to the painful event as if it happened yesterday. Emotions don't evaporate and go away. They must be dealt with. The tragedy must, as it were, be revisited and lived through. Only then can life go on in a healthy way. Without going through the pain and darkness — deny it as we might — we cannot go on. Denial, like the body's production of pain-numbing endorphins, is intended only as a momentary relief, until such time as we can face what happened.

A Lesson Learned While Eavesdropping

In 1969, when I was a pastoral intern at Lutheran Medical Center in Brooklyn, New York, I was assigned the task of ministering to a woman who was dying of cancer. The first time I went to her room, filled with the apprehension and dread that comes with inexperience, I saw that her children were in the hospital room with her. I stood outside the door, unsure of what to do. No one had seen me, but I could hear them talking. The children, all of whom were adults, kept assuring and reassuring their mother that she was going to be fine, that she was going to come through this and be her old self.

My eavesdropping that day was the best introduction to the power of denial I could have had as a young student. I could sense how panic-stricken the children were at the prospect of losing their mother. They needed her to stay alive. All of their assurances were meant not for their mother but for themselves. It was as if they were saying, "We can't deal with the prospect of Mother's death, so we will ignore what the doctors say and her obvious physical

70

deterioration and pretend it isn't really happening." That's a perfectly understandable thing for children to do. The fact that their mother was dying may have taken them back to childhood and the terrible fright of being abandoned by the one who was their protector and nurturer, and such fright perhaps was simply too much to contend with emotionally. The pain was simply too great.

When the family had left I went in and introduced myself. After we had gotten to know each other a little, I looked into her eyes and said, "You're dying, aren't you?" How I had the guts to do that as a rookie, I have no idea. I also had no idea what her reaction would be. Perhaps she would order me out of the room and never allow me back in, or complain to my supervisor. In fact, the opposite occurred. A look of relief came over her face and it appeared that a horrible weight had been lifted from her shoulders. Finally the truth had been spoken and she was ready to deal with it, even though her children weren't. All she said to me was, "Thank you." Then we talked about dying: the terrible fright associated with death, her worries about how her children would cope, and all the rest of it. I don't know what became of her or her children. I do know that for a moment, at least, she was able to face her situation without blinders. Perhaps that made it possible for her to help her children deal constructively with what was coming.

This brief encounter taught me that keeping up appearances can be the most difficult work in the world. The power of denial, as important to our sanity as it initially is, can become a burden too heavy to carry. We can become addicted to denial in exactly the way that we become addicted to pain pills. They protect us from pain, but they don't help us deal with it constructively. In fact, in the long run denial and painkillers can prevent us from dealing with psychic and physical pain at all. Denial is the most powerful narcotic available to us, and it's free and perfectly legal.

The Happiest Place On Earth

A life constructed on the foundation of denial is illusory and ultimately destructive, because we end up creating a fantasy life that, like Disneyland, is supposed to be the happiest place on earth. Fantasies filter out anything that is negative. The focus is on fun

71

and self-indulgence. (And, of course, the vendors at Disneyland are happy to relieve you of your money at tremendously inflated prices while you are in your happy stupor.) I might enjoy myself for a while, but after wandering around Disneyland for an hour or two, being hit in the shins by strollers and jostled by crowds intent on having the best time ever, I'm ready to leave. Being in a theme park sooner or later becomes a matter of the survival of the fittest.

You don't have to go to Disneyland to see the power of denial at work. The lure and promise of denial permeate and drive nearly every aspect of American culture. It underlies all advertising. The promise is that if you have a new car, a streamlined body, a new house, the right job, the right clothes, membership in the right club, friends who think as you do, and whatever else Madison Avenue thinks you need, then you will be happy. And it isn't just the advertising world that gets into the denial business; the churches do it as well. The message one often hears is that if you really have faith, if you think positively, if you keep anything negative from ever entering your awareness, then you will be happy — as God intended you to be!

Unfortunately, the corollary is that if you don't have all this, if you aren't happy and fulfilled, you simply aren't trying hard enough! Once again, the burden is placed on you. You can do it if only you try. You can pull yourself up by your own bootstraps — at least you had better be able to, because everything depends on *you*!

Although it worked for socially isolated people on the frontier a century and a half ago, the spirit of frontier rugged individualism spells the death of community. Rugged individuals cannot reach out to others. The individualistic code of conduct does not allow for that. You either sink or swim by yourself. If you sink, there probably won't be anyone around to mourn your disappearance. And if you succeed, no one will applaud you either, because we're all too busy trying to keep our own heads above water.

Individualism is not a social glue that holds people together. Individualism is more akin to dynamite. It shatters any notion of corporate life. We're all on our own. Happiness, when it occurs, can only be my happiness. Tragedy, when it occurs, can only be mine as well.

Rugged individualism is the illusion relentlessly pursued by us in North America. But is Scripture about rugged individualism, or is it about community? Disneyland promotes the fulfillment of individuals, all of whom are jostling each other and running into each other in the crazed pursuit of fun. There is no sense of community there. It's about *me*! As such, Disneyland is a microcosm of American society.

James Luther Adams defined meaning in life as "a shared and enjoyed relatedness."[40] Meaning and happiness are empty concepts unless they occur between and among people. To be sure, there are people who enjoy their splendid isolation. Yet even they have memory and imagination, both of which are "peopled," as it were. To have the capacity for language means that there is some part of our being that thrives on communication. And to communicate is to relate, even if such relations are with those remembered or those imagined.

The American obsession with communication technology suggests that our need for connection with others is very powerful. E-mail is convenient, but it does not satisfy our hunger for another human voice — and not a recorded voice that lists a myriad of options, either! There appears to be in us rugged individuals a great hunger for internal relatedness, for intimacy.

There are plenty of superficial, external relationships available to us, among which television is the most ubiquitous. The characters on television influence and affect us by what they say and do, but we cannot affect them. The relationship flows one way only — from them to us. The program and their lives go on with or without us.

By contrast, an internal relationship is one in which the persons mutually affect each other. The relationship flows back and forth. In this kind of relationship it really does matter if one person is not there. If James Luther Adams is right, it is only here that meaning and happiness are to be found.

The Theology Of Glory

Martin Luther called anything that promises complete fulfillment in this life a theology of glory. Such a theology assumes that we can have heaven on earth, that we can create Utopia (this Greek word literally means "no place"). Any theology of glory requires that we ignore huge segments of experience that don't fit our utopian dreams. Suffering, pain, and death certainly have no place in such dreams. These simply cannot be allowed in "The Happiest Place on Earth." Any theology of glory requires that we live in denial, like the children who couldn't accept the fact that their mother was actually dying of cancer.

How does the theology of glory show itself? What forms does it take? The most common form is the idea that life is getting progressively better and better. "God is in his heaven; all is right with the world." This supposition has lain at the roots of American life from its inception. America, in the minds of thinkers in eighteenth-century Europe, was to be humanity's great second chance to get things right. America was conceived of as the new Garden of Eden and Americans as the new Adams and Eves. Whatever else Americans would do, they would certainly avoid the errors of their European forebears. And, of course, California, the Golden State, has long been thought of as the place of new beginnings.

John Steinbeck's novel *The Grapes of Wrath* is concerned with the displaced tenant farmers in Oklahoma in the Dust Bowl of the 1930s who went to California with the expectation of finding Utopia. Jobs would be plentiful. If you wanted fruit, you could just pick it off the trees in your yard. The sun always shines in California and everyone is happy all the time. But what the Oklahoma migrants actually encountered in California was very much like what they had left in Oklahoma. Workers were taken advantage of, lied to, cheated, and even killed, when they attempted to organize fruit pickers into unions. The hard lesson of *The Grapes of Wrath* is that Utopia doesn't exist in the Golden State any more than it existed on the East Coast or in Europe. Utopia is a pipe dream.

So the question becomes: What will we do if we can't create a perfect world, if we can't do away with pain, suffering, and death? How can we live in an imperfect world without becoming cynical about life?

Here the theology of glory — the positive outlook — is of no help at all. We can think as positively as we want, but we can't do away with the hard realities of life — all the things brought into our homes by the daily news. We might adopt the definition of luck given by the ancient Greeks: "Luck is when the arrow hits the guy next to you." And our luck might hold out for a long time, but eventually the arrow hits us in one way or another — perhaps by illness, the death of a loved one, the loss of a job, or the fact that we will die. And when the arrow hits us, as it inevitably will, what will sustain us? We could, of course, take Scarlet O'Hara's attitude in *Gone with the Wind* and say, "I'll think about it tomorrow." Eventually, however, tomorrow comes. We might even use Ebenezer Scrooge's tack and say that the ghost of Jacob Marley, who warns Scrooge of dire things to come, is nothing but a bit of undigested beef.

It's Easier To Be An Optimist
If You Don't Actually See The World
Following World War II there was a cartoon in the daily papers called *Little Orphan Annie*. Annie, who was apparently orphaned by the war, wore a perpetual smile on her face and was always happy. This was possible because she had no pupils in her eyes! She couldn't see what was actually happening around her. The message of the cartoon seemed to be that you, too, can be perpetually happy. The secret of such happiness is to take no notice of what is actually going on in and around yourself.

The message of religion in America is the same. We are admonished to think positively. Norman Vincent Peale and his protégé Robert Schuler have been the high priests of positive thinking for a long time and they have many disciples, a number of whom make a good living from the message. These preachers become models for listeners. The real message (never spoken, of course) is, "If you heed well what I say, you too can be on top of the world — just like me. Oh, and by the way, send money." And it works! People send money by the truckload, even if it means that they have to live on popcorn. There is something in us that needs desperately to believe that the message of positive thinking really works.

Faith Goes Beyond Optimism And Pessimism

But how can we take life in its fullness seriously if we have to live by the illusion that everything will be all right if only we believe hard enough? How can we absorb the onslaught of negative experiences and not be destroyed by it? How can we get beyond the shallow categories of optimism and pessimism as if these were the only options available to us? How, in short, can we learn to live hopefully in the real world, the world as it actually is?

The theology of the cross is much older than the Reformers. It can be found in the Old Testament in the books of Isaiah, Jeremiah, Ecclesiastes, and many of the Psalms. It is at the very heart and core of the New Testament in the four Gospels and the letters of Paul. The *theologia crucis* (theology of the cross) is the opposite of the *theologia gloriae* (theology of glory). In a debate held in the German city of Heidelberg in 1518, Luther, a 35-year-old Augustinian monk, startled his older contemporaries with this statement, "A theologian of glory calls evil good and good evil. A theologian of the cross calls the thing what it actually is." They had never heard anything like this before!

We can take as a clue to what Luther meant the saying of Jesus, "A disciple is not above the teacher, nor a slave above the master; it is enough for the disciple to be like the teacher, and the slave like the master" (Matthew 10:24). In other words, the experience of Jesus will also be our experience. This will include suffering and death. Instead of living lives of denial, however, we can dare enter the darkness of our world, because, as Canadian theologian Douglas John Hall says, when we enter the darkness we meet the one who is the light of the world (*Christus lux mundi*, Christ the light of the world).[41] Jesus reveals himself to us in the darkness, those places in ourselves and in the world where suffering occurs.

The theology of glory teaches us that we find happiness only as we avoid suffering and keep up the appearance that everything's fine. Is that what Jesus taught? He said things like, "Take up your cross and follow me." The entire New Testament points us to a crucified Jesus, which we must do everything in our power not to notice if we want to be "happy." Or we conveniently skip over the crucifixion and run to Easter Sunday, as popular preachers today do, and grab on desperately to the resurrection. What we don't realize is that the resurrection cannot be had without the crucifixion. The fact is that we live in a world with the stamp of Good Friday on it, a world battered by the forces of destruction. The twentieth century was the deadliest century in human history and the twenty-first century has the potential of being even deadlier. The very technology we look to for salvation, for the solution of all our problems, has a forebodingly dark side. The technology that "saves" is also capable of utterly annihilating life on earth. One of the greatest challenges facing us today is what to do with nuclear waste, the "leftovers" from a nuclear technology that provides us with cheap electricity. Moreover, the European and American ways of life are rapidly depleting the world's natural resources and destroying the oceans and the atmosphere, while 90 percent of the world's population live in conditions we would never put up with. We can maintain our way of life and our positive outlook only by denying these realities.

Faith Is Realistic About The Way The World Is

Christian faith, said Reinhold Niebuhr, is the ability to see reality as it actually is, but without falling into despair.[42] Christian faith is neither optimism nor pessimism. It is realistic about the way the world is. It goes deeper into reality, into the way experience truly is, than either optimism or pessimism would dare to go and discovers that Christ is present in the darkest places — although in hidden form. This is the Christ who cried out in terror, "My God, my God, why have you forsaken me?" Christ has gone into the deepest recesses of the world's darkness. This is what we mean when we confess in The Apostles' Creed, "And he descended into hell." Hell is the place of absolute Godforsakenness. No place, no matter how dark, is unknown to him.

We therefore can dare to enter the places of suffering into which experience thrusts us in the confidence that we will never be abandoned there. We can dare to listen to what the darkness has to teach us rather than always running from it. We can sit with those who suffer without having to provide answers to why this is happening. Suffering doesn't go away, even if and when answers are found for what is occurring. Suffering is lessened, however, by the willingness of another person simply to be with us in that particular time and place of darkness.

The God rediscovered by the Reformers is the God of predestination. Contrary to popular opinion, predestination is not the same thing as philosophical determinism. It has nothing to do with a God who manipulates us like puppets on strings. Predestination means that God goes before us (pre-) to give us a destiny (destination). God did this in the life, death, and resurrection of Jesus of Nazareth. Here death does not have the final word. Instead, life has the final word.

And now we can state the difference between optimism and hope. Hope is what comes into being when optimism has come to an end. Optimism is fragile. It can easily be shattered if we are at all aware of what happens to us on a daily basis. Optimism requires that we blot out large portions of the world and of our experience — that we ignore what is actually going on around us. Optimism requires that we create Utopia.

Hope, on the other hand, is able to take the world as it is (and not as we would like it to be) without falling into despair and cynicism. Hope can do this because it lives from the promises of God, the God who did not abandon his Son to suffering, death, and hell. The fact that God raised Jesus from the dead and will do the same to us gives us the confidence *that it's not all up to us*. We are actors in a drama that is much larger than we are. It is a drama that includes comedy and tragedy. It is a drama in which we have creative roles to play in making and keeping human life human and of caring for the creation. We are not, however, the main actors. That role belongs to Christ alone who, in his own time and way, will make all things new. Therefore we can do the work that lies before us in the courage and conviction that what we do will be taken up into the larger work of God, who continues to bring light out of darkness and life out of death.

This brings us to a question of what it means to be the church today, a discussion that will include a definition of the church and its mission to a world that, although battered and beaten daily, nonetheless remains the creation of God.

Chapter Five

What Is The Church?

The Word Of God

The church belongs to Jesus Christ. He is the architect, builder, and cornerstone of the church. It does not and never has belonged to us. The Spirit of God (that is, God present with us in hidden fashion) works through the church, but the Spirit is not limited to the church. The Spirit blows where it will and is not accountable to us. Can God save those outside the church? Of course! But God has chosen to work through the church as well, and that is our focus as Christian disciples.

Apart from the Word of God there is no church. The Bible is the witness of the historical confessors of the faith, confessors who handed over the tradition to us. We, as the disciple community, have been entrusted with a story that is ancient, but which has not lost its ability to grasp the hearts and minds of people even now. We are the custodians of this precious story.

The Word of God is creative. It creates a new reality. "In the beginning when God created the heavens and the earth, the earth was a formless void and darkness covered the face of the deep, while a wind from God swept over the face of the waters. Then God said, 'Let there be light'; and there was light" (Genesis 1:1-3, NRSV). Something that had not existed (light) was called into being by God speaking a word.

When we think of the Word of God, it is the Bible that usually comes to mind. But Luther knew that it is more than that. The Word of God is first and foremost Jesus Christ, the Word made flesh, the incarnate Word. Only then is it Scripture, preaching, and sacraments. The Bible is the written Word of God; preaching is the spoken Word of God; and the sacraments are the visible Word of God.

Jesus As The Word Of God

In the New Testament, Jesus is called the Word of God. "In the beginning was the Word, and the Word was with God, and the Word was God. All things came into being through him, and without him not one thing came into being. What has come into being in him was life, and the life was the light of all people. The light shines in the darkness, and the darkness did not overcome it" (John 1:1-5, NRSV).

The similarities between the opening verses of Genesis and those of John are obvious. Both begin with the phrase "In the beginning...." John is making the statement that the creative Word that brought light out of darkness at the creation of the universe was Jesus himself. "All things came into being through him [the pre-existent Jesus], and without him not one thing came into being" (John 1:3).

Such a connection is made time after time in the New Testament. In the familiar story of the storm at sea in Mark 4:35-41, Jesus and the disciples are on the Sea of Galilee in a fishing boat at night. He is asleep in the back of the boat. The wind begins to blow, the waves build up and crash against the small craft, and the disciples are terrified that the boat will sink and that they will all drown. "Teacher, do you not care that we are perishing?" they cry out. And with that "he rebuked the wind, and said to the sea, 'Peace! Be still!' Then the wind ceased, and there was a dead calm." (The Greek carries the connotation, "Shut up! That's enough!") With the onset of the sudden calm, the disciples are even more frightened than they were during the storm. "And they were filled with great awe and said to one another, 'Who then is this, that even the wind and the sea obey him?' " The implication of this story is that, through Jesus, the disciples were being encountered by the one who said in the beginning, "Let there be light!"

In the ancient world, the sea, with its great depths and its unpredictability, symbolized the power of chaos and death — the very forces that ruled before the creation. Here — and later, when Jesus walks on the water (Mark 6:47-51) — he is shown to be the one who is greater than death. He not only silences the power of death but actually walks on it as though it were nothing. These incidents are glimpses of the final victory over death, the resurrection. The arbitrary kingdom of death has been invaded by one who is stronger.

Death prevailed on Good Friday. But once again God spoke at the tomb of his Son and said, "Let there be light!" and there was light. Jesus was raised from the bonds of death, never again to be its victim.

The Word of God is first and foremost Jesus Christ. He is the Word made flesh (John 1:14). Apart from Jesus of Nazareth, we can know nothing of God. All we can do is speculate about what God might or might not be like. The witness of nature is ambiguous at best: nature is beautiful, but it can also terrifyingly destructive. In Jesus of Nazareth we see the very heart of God. And what is it that we see? We see him feeding the hungry, healing the sick, raising the dead, comforting the afflicted, and casting out demons. In other words, we see him creating new life wherever the enemies of life (hunger, illness, death, affliction, and demonic possession) are at work. "In him was life, and the life was the light of all people" (John 1:4).

Scripture, Preaching, And Sacraments As The Word Of God

The Word of God in a secondary or derivative sense is the Bible (the written Word), preaching (the spoken Word), and the sacraments of Baptism and Holy Communion (the visible Word). These are the means through which Jesus is made present among us, the means by which the Spirit of God (*Spiritus Creator*) creates faith and new life in us. As we read the words of the Bible, as we hear the Bible expounded in preaching, as we receive the water of Baptism and the bread and wine of Communion, something new happens. The Word of God in all of its forms does something to us. It kills and makes alive. The Word of God puts to death in us that which is in bondage to sin and unbelief and raises up people who trust God above all else and who love the things that make for life.

How does this happen? Whenever the Law stops us dead in our tracks and we are brought to the point of confession of our sins and receive the forgiveness of sins, we have gone through a death and resurrection. Confession is a dying. It is the recognition that we are not perfect, that we indeed are not God. It is the recognition that we are flawed — fatally flawed. Absolution is the rising to new life. To use the ancient term, we are sinful, but we are at the same time the beloved children of God. This fact is what makes life possible for imperfect creatures who live in an imperfect world.

Dietrich Bonhoeffer, the budding German theologian who was executed for his part in a plot to assassinate Hitler, said that none of us gets out of this world with clean hands. Our best efforts, our noblest efforts carry with them the taint of self-interest. Only physical death and resurrection to new life will cure the sickness unto death (to use Kierkegaard's term), which is self-interest.

In the meantime we do what we can to make and keep human life human — as imperfect as those efforts are. The fact that they are imperfect does not mean that they are useless. It only means that they are provisional (the Latin *providere* means to see [*videre*] ahead [*pro*]), that is, our actions look ahead to or anticipate God's actions on behalf of humanity and the world. God will take up our imperfect work and perfect it.

The Church

The reformers defined the church as "the assembly of all believers among whom the gospel is purely preached and the holy sacraments are administered according to the gospel."[43] Wherever the gospel is preached and the sacraments are administered, there is the church, whether that is in a beautiful building or in a vacant lot. It is the Word of God that creates the church. It belongs to Christ alone. And its purpose and mission are to see to it that the gospel is proclaimed and the sacraments are administered. If the church does not proclaim the justification of the godless, who will?

The gospel is meant for the world, for God's good creation that has turned its back on God. The gospel is God's "I love you" to the world. And if God so loves the world, how can the church turn its back on the world? If God became human to take up residence in the world, how can the church turn a deaf ear and an unseeing eye to the suffering of the world?

The gospel propels us into the world, into the pain and suffering of those around us. Spiritual care is doing the things Jesus did:

healing the sick, feeding the hungry, comforting those who are in distress, and confronting the demons that threaten to destroy the creation and thrust us back into the primordial darkness and chaos: racism, hunger, oppression, hopelessness, and all the other demonic powers that threaten to undo us.

Martin Luther in his *Large Catechism* wrote:

> *Therefore, it [Holy Communion] is appropriately called food of the soul, for it nourishes and strengthens the new creature. For in the first instance, we are born anew through baptism. However, our human flesh and blood, as I have said, have not lost their old skin. There are so many hindrances and attacks of the devil and the world that we often grow weary and faint and at times even stumble. Therefore the Lord's Supper is given as a daily food and sustenance so that our faith may be refreshed and strengthened and that it may not succumb in the struggle but become stronger and stronger. For the new life should be one that continually develops and progresses. But it has to suffer a great deal of opposition. The devil is a furious enemy; when he sees that we resist him and attack the old creature, and when he cannot rout us by force, he sneaks and skulks about at every turn, trying all kinds of tricks, and does not stop until he has finally worn us out so that we either renounce our faith or lose heart and become indifferent and impatient. For times like these, when our heart feels too sorely pressed, this comfort of the Lord's Supper is given to bring us new strength and refreshment.*[44]

The Church And The Kingdom Of God

We are up against principalities and powers, as Paul says in Romans 8:38. What we read about in the press and see so graphically on television newscasts — kids killing kids, babies having babies, corporations looking after the bottom line rather than the welfare of workers, the wanton destruction of the earth's resources, wars and rumors of wars, and on and on — are evidences of the destructive powers that the ancient tradition has called the devil. If that term is too archaic, we can certainly use the term "demonic"

83

without stretching our imaginations. All of us get caught up in those things that make for death rather than life. And it is against these that the church is poised.

The contemporary Dutch theologian Edward Schillebeeckx says that the church is the germ and the beginning of the kingdom of God on earth, but that the church always exists under shadows.[45] That is to say, the church is not the kingdom of God, but points to that kingdom as a future reality. The church falls prey to the temptations of power and influence, like other institutions in society. The church becomes involved in self-promotion and self-adulation. It succumbs to the spirit of self-importance and boosterism. These are the shadows Schillebeeckx speaks of.

When the world looks at the church, however, it should see not a mirror image of itself but its future. In Karl Rahner's terms, the church is the sign of the salvation of the world (*sacramentum salutis totius mundi*). As Christ is the salvation of all people — those who lived before him as well as after him — so the church is the promise of salvation to the world of all ages.[46] It is the promise of that future. This is not to say that the future kingdom of God exists only in the future. The kingdom of God, to which the church points and witnesses, is also present in hidden fashion wherever the Spirit of Christ is present.

To say that the kingdom is hidden means that its presence is not obvious but that we nonetheless get intimations now and again of God's presence with us. We see it in the newness of life that is given in the forgiveness of sins, that is, in the sacraments. In his *Small Catechism* Luther says regarding the words "given and shed for you for the remission of sins" in Holy Communion: "These words assure us that in the sacrament we receive forgiveness of sins, life, and salvation. *For where there is forgiveness of sins, there is also life and salvation.*"

Salvation is a reality here and now. It comes in the form of new life that is beyond our ability to create: the surprising and unexpected presence of love in a situation that has been characterized by hatred; acceptance of ourselves as deeply loved in spite of all those things we dislike about ourselves; the birth of a passion for life just when we had given up on the whole human enterprise;

84

the ability to see beyond prejudice, which enables us to see the enemy as human beings who possess fears and longings very much like our own.

The miraculous appearance of such unexpected newness is what saves us from spiraling down into cynicism and despair. "Love," Paul Tillich wrote, "is the power of the new in every man and in all history. It cannot age; it removes guilt and curse. It is working even today toward new creation. It is hidden in the darkness of our souls and of our history. But it is not completely hidden to those who are grasped by its reality."[47]

When we pray in the Lord's Prayer, "Thy kingdom come, thy will be done on earth as it is in Heaven," we are praying for the return of Jesus who, when he does return, will recreate us and the universe, so that everything will be as God first intended it. Then all things will be new. The power and principalities will at last be vanquished. There will be no more death, hunger, or violence. Nature itself will be at peace and we will live in harmony with nature and with one another, as it was intended "in the beginning." Then God's will shall be done on earth as it is now done in heaven.

What this will be like is beautifully described in Isaiah 11:6-9:

The wolf shall live with the lamb,
and the leopard shall lie down with the kid,
and the calf and the lion and the fatling together,
and a little child shall lead them.
The cow and the bear shall graze,
their young shall lie down together;
and the lion shall eat straw like the ox.
The nursing child shall play over the hole of the asp,
and the weaned child shall put his hand on the adder's den.
They will not hurt or destroy in all my holy mountain;
for the earth shall be full of the knowledge of the Lord
as the waters cover the sea.

This vision of Isaiah's has been rendered by many artists under the title "The Peaceable Kingdom." Natural enemies are portrayed as living at peace with each other. Infants play with poisonous snakes and are not harmed by them. This is what it will be like when the Messiah returns. For Jesus, the great lion of the tribe of Judah (recall C. S. Lewis's portrayal of Jesus as the great lion Aslan), as the book of Revelation describes him, is the death of death. The resurrection of Jesus means that death has been destroyed. It continues to rage against us, but its days are numbered.

Viewed sociologically, the church will always be one human institution among many others. Viewed theologically, however, the church signifies the world's future, the fact that the world is cherished as the creation by the one who first created it. In and through the church, the world should be able to hear God's "I love you" as an address to the world, even and especially when the world says, "No!" to God. The church, says Karl Rahner, pursues a pilgrim way in the world; that is, a way that needs to be different from the world's way. If the world's way is obsession with itself, the church points to the coming kingdom of God as the better way. The church is always pointing away from itself to the coming kingdom of Christ, the peaceable kingdom, as God's intention for the world.

The Church Under The Cross (*Ecclesia Crucis*)

Douglas John Hall describes the church as being under the cross, as the *ecclesia crucis*. When the church understands itself properly, says Hall, it will give up dreams of creating empires and will cease cozying up to governments. The church under the cross pursues faithfulness to the Crucified. It is to be in the world, but not of it. Hall believes we are living at the end of the historical epoch when government and church legitimate each other. This has been the case since Emperor Constantine made Christianity the favored religion of the Roman Empire. The history of the relationship since then has been one of bishops crowning emperors and kings and monarchs granting special privileges to the church. Whether we realize it or not, Hall argues, that era has ended. Now the church is on its own.[48]

In this new situation the church must learn to live not from the benefits and privileges of government but from the promises of God. The church must learn to identify with and cast its lot with those who have been trampled by the powerful. The church has the opportunity at last to be the church of the Crucified One, who numbered himself among the outcasts of society.

In Reformation teaching the church is the place where the gospel is preached and the sacraments are rightly administered. It is not there for any other reason. The church is discovered in acts of liberation. Gerhard Forde writes,

> *Where the message of freedom and hope is proclaimed, where it is given to you and sealed by sacramental action, there you are reached and touched by the true church. What is hidden is revealed! The true church is made up of those liberated by the good news. It is the communion of believers, the bearer of the proclamation of freedom and hope.*[49]

The church exists for the world, which means that it may have to take up stances against the world. When the world says it is all right to rape the earth in order to maintain the American way of life, the church must speak a resounding "No!" We are called to make common cause with others who advocate for the creation. When the world embraces racism, the church says, "No!" And we must say it, not just with our voices but with our very lives. When the world says it's all right for millions of people to be hungry every day, the church must say, "No!" It is not all right for a few to embrace most of the world's riches. By standing against the world in these and any number of other ways, the church acts on behalf of the world.

The world is not to be despised, nor is it to be uncritically embraced. What good does it do for the church to withdraw from what goes on in the world? What good does it do for the church simply to mimic the world? The relationship between the church and world must be a dialectical one, a relationship of give-and-take. The church has a great deal to learn from the world, and the world has a great deal to learn from the church. Whether they can do so is the challenge today. Forde puts it this way:

> *The church is that community which bears witness to the end, the goal of human life. It declares that that*

end, God's kingdom to come, is the gift entirely of grace. Because it is a gift of grace, we are set free to live a down-to-earth existence, to wait patiently and to combat all those things which tempt men to betray the hope — the wiles of the devil, the world, the flesh. To be in the church is to take up this battle in this world.[50]

Chapter Six

Fiat Iustitia (Let There Be Justice)

The Struggle For Human Righteousness

The Reformers made an important distinction between human and divine righteousness. The righteousness of God is that which only God can bestow on human beings. The love of God for us is shown by the fact that God makes us righteous (recall the discussion of justification in chapter 3, above). This is a pure gift, which none of us can merit or expect as a reward for a life well lived. The story the Bible tells is not a story of human greatness. From Adam and Eve on, the story has been one of human rebellion against God. In spite of this, God shows his love for us in that while we were yet sinners (that is, while we were still alienated from God) Christ died for the *ungodly* (Romans 5:6f).

The Reformation made it clear that we are not saved by our good works. Ever since then, however, the problem has been what to make of good works. Luther himself had no difficulty with this. He said very clearly that good works are intended for our neighbors and for the good earth. Good works do not get us to heaven, but they are nonetheless important for life here and now. In fact, Luther, arguing against those in the Reformation movement who saw no value in good works, said they could call him "Dr. Good Works."

Good works are what make life in this world possible. A father is closest to God, said Luther, when he changes his daughter's dirty diapers. In and of itself, changing dirty diapers is not a pleasant task — but it is a life-sustaining task, an act of the pure love, even when it must be done in the middle of the night when you would much rather be asleep. Without such acts of sacrifice and love, life would grind to a halt. So Luther never tired of saying that God does not need our good works, but our neighbor does.

To speak of good works, of morality, is to speak of sacrifice. The moral life is a life of sacrifice on behalf of another. Sacrifice involves the loss of something important to me in order that someone else might benefit. Parents make sacrifices for their children all the time, and children do the same for their parents. We sacrifice willingly for someone we love. And when the sacrifice grows out of love for another, we don't even think of it as a sacrifice. We might even make sacrifices for someone we don't love, which is rare but not unheard of.

In the same spirit, Karl Barth (1886-1968) asserts that "Christians are claimed for action in the effort and struggle for human righteousness. At issue is human, not divine righteousness."[51] In other words, our task is not to create the kingdom of God on earth, something that God alone can and will do when Jesus returns. Our task is not to create Utopia, which has been attempted — often with disastrous results. The task before us is much more modest: to band with others to make and keep human life human.[52]

The Things Above And The Things Below

In the things above, which have to do with God and with salvation, we have no free will. Here good works are of no avail. God elects or chooses us quite apart from our willing or doing anything ("You did not choose me, but I chose you," John 15:16). In matters of salvation we have no part to play.

In the things below, which have to do with this life, we do have free will, and what we do matters greatly. These things have to do with the welfare of our neighbor and the well-being of nature. History shows that the human record in this respect is quite dismal, involving a series of wars and the despoliation of nature, to mention only two things.

In our common life on earth we are commissioned to live creatively rather than destructively, to bend our efforts in the direction of life rather than death. We are to be, in Douglas John Hall's words, stewards of life in the kingdom of death.[53] To be created in the image of God means to participate in the creative work of God, the work of the Creator Spirit. God did not end his creative work with the creation of the universe. The Spirit of God, which hovered over the chaos in the beginning, continues to work, to create. The creation did not happen all at once. It is an ongoing project.

To participate in the creative work of God is to be a steward of life. A steward is one who looks after that which belongs to someone else, who tends it and safeguards it. This stewardship reflects itself in the struggle for justice. This, as Luther says, means a "life spent profitably in good works."[54] God does not need our good works, but our neighbors and the creation do.

In this work we are not masters of the situation; we cannot solve all problems for all time. But this in no way detracts from the importance of our work as stewards of life. Jesus did not heal everyone, did not feed everyone, did not even raise all the dead — and neither will we. As a church under the sign of the cross (*ecclesia crucis*), we can be in the world as friends of those who also suffer in the world. What does that mean?

What Do We Really Think About This World?

To be friends of the suffering means, first, overcoming the temptation to write the world off and to occupy ourselves only with heaven. If Jesus didn't do that, why should we? The fact that God became human shows that the world is critically important to God. It is still God's good creation, which he loves. "And God saw all that he had made, and behold it was very good" (Genesis 1:31). "God so loved *the world* ..." (John 3:16). We do not have the luxury of considering the world to be of no importance.

It is tempting to give up on the world if only because the problems are so immense, so staggering, so seemingly immune to remedy. Suffering persists in spite of our best medical technology. Poverty persists in spite of Lyndon Johnson's war on poverty forty years ago. The poor continue to die on the streets of Calcutta and of every other city in the world in spite of a lifetime of work by Mother Teresa. Racism persists in America in spite of the tremendous impact of Martin Luther King, Jr. War, pollution, and every other destructive pursuit of human greed persist in spite of our best efforts to eliminate them. Why *should* we persist in our efforts to seek that which makes for life? Why not abandon a sinking ship?

Abandoning life in this world is not an option because of the one whom we follow. Jesus' call is in the imperative: "Follow me." It is not a suggestion; it is a command. We learn faith, Dietrich

Bonhoeffer says, by actually following Jesus. We don't wait for faith so that we can then follow. We follow and by so doing learn faith.

> As long as Levi sits in the tax collector's booth and Peter at his nets, they would do their work honestly and loyally, they would have old or new knowledge about God. But if they want to learn to believe in God, they have to follow the Son of God incarnate and walk with him.[55]

Bonhoeffer's understanding of trust in Jesus as an outgrowth of following him grew out of Bonhoeffer's life-and-death struggle with Nazism. It would have been far safer to say nothing in opposition to the Nazis — to play the game, so to speak. Indeed, Bonhoeffer could have stayed at Union Seminary in New York City and taught there in safety. But he knew he had to go back to Germany and take up the fight against Hitler and the Christians who chose to conform to Nazi ideology. "[F]aith exists only in obedience, is never without obedience. Faith is only faith in deeds of obedience."[56]

Attempting to find ways to motivate ourselves to action on behalf of others and on behalf of the creation could go on forever. One can attempt to learn to swim by reading books about the techniques involved in swimming, but at some point one simply has to get wet to find out what swimming is really about.

The Passion For Life

Being friends of those who suffer means, second, having passion for life here and now. What motivated Dietrich Bonhoeffer and Martin Luther King, Jr., was a passion for life, a passionate caring about what was going on around them. What is the source of such passion? It is the Spirit of God. As a mother cares passionately about her children and will make any sacrifice to insure their safety and well-being, so God cares passionately about this world, his good creation — even to the point of being destroyed by the world. That kind of passion grows as we immerse ourselves in the life of the world — to the point of loving the world in spite of its craziness.

We are, after all, intimately related to the world. The Hebrew name Adam (man) comes from *adamah* (soil). Contemporary German theologian Jürgen Moltmann writes:

> *Human life is alive to the extent that it is loved and affirmed. The more passionately we love life, the more intensively we experience the joy of life. The more passionately we love life, the more we also experience the pain of life and the deadliness of death. We experience joy and pain, we become alive and mortal at one and the same time, not simply in life, but in that interest in life we call love.*[57]

And then Moltmann makes this fascinating statement:

> *Death is hopeless — and therefore horrible — only where life has not been lived and loved. What oppresses us in the hour of death, therefore, is not the life that has been lived and loved, but rather the life that has not been lived and that has neglected its possibilities. Only the passion of love makes a person alive right down to the very fingertips. At the same time it makes a person able and ready to die.*[58]

The Life Of Discipleship

Life in North America has been shaped by the idea of progress. The expectation formed by the idea of progress is that history is moving toward perfection. "Every day and in every way, things are getting better and better." And the means by which everything improves day by day is technology. The expectation is that with the right tools and the right expertise every problem can be solved. But to maintain such a perspective on history we must become blind to tragic occurrences in our individual and common lives. And we choose not to see that which doesn't fit with our ideas about progress, because we don't know how to deal with people, things, and events than can't be fixed.

93

Can we dare to enter the dark places of our own lives and of our common life without having to solve everything, without having to be masters of the situation? Can we enter those difficult places with the hope that we will be met by the one who is the light of the world? This is what taking up our cross and following Jesus means. We encounter the darkness not as experts but as followers of the one who has gone there before us. We go into the dark places as those who are not surprised by the fact that tragic events happen, but also as those who have learned to trust the promise of God to make all things new (Revelation 21:5). This promise of God is the basis of our hope — not any presumed expertise of our own.

Of course, we do what we can to make life better for others. There is a great deal that is in our control. But we also recognize our limits. There is a great deal that is not in our control. And we will not always agree on the best means for making life better. Our hope has been in technology to do this, but we also know that technology has a very dark side to it. We won't agree on answers to questions arising from genetic technology, just as we have not agreed about the other staggering ethical issues of our day.

Justice is not always easily or quickly attainable. In this world justice is most often defined by those who have political and economic power. Justice is whatever is good for them. Disciples of Jesus, the powerless one, should learn to look for definitions of what is good, right, just, and beautiful from those individuals and groups who are outside the halls of power. What would happen if we began looking to those on the margins of society for help in defining these things? Do the poor know something about happiness that the rich know nothing of? Do those who have had no access to education know things that might be of great help to us who are educated?

Discipleship is an adventure. It takes us to places and places us among people with whom we might not normally associate. There are no pure and innocent groups of people in the world, no groups with all the answers to every question. But what an interesting thing it could be to strike up conversations with those who are vastly different from us to see what we might learn from each other.

Conclusion

What Difference Does It Make?

The stories narrated by the Bible are thousands of years old.
The Reformation occurred 500 years ago. How can any of it matter today? Why not listen to new, contemporary voices and let the
past be the past? We Americans have never been patient with the
study of history. We are far too busy creating the future. Paul Tillich,
who was forced by Hitler's government to leave Germany in the
late 1930s because he defended his Jewish colleagues against the
attacks of the Nazis, came to America and was immediately impressed with how little we value the past. He said that the bulldozer is the symbol of America. The old is always being knocked
down in order to make room for the new. So why should we listen
to voices of the past, and the Reformers' voices in particular?

I am convinced that especially Martin Luther's authentic voice
has not really been heard in America. His theology, to be sure, has
been taught in seminaries and churches, but it is so radically different from what Americans are used to hearing that it runs off our
backs, like water off a duck. It continues not to find a home among
us. The situation is not so different from Dietrich Bonhoeffer's
experience in New York in the 1930s.

If all we as the church have to say to the world is, "Try harder!"
or, "Heaven is yours if you can qualify for it and have done your
part to deserve it," then we have not even come close to the Bible
or to the Reformation. The Reformation of the sixteenth century
was an explosion. It shattered the unity of the medieval church and
the political status quo of Europe. But it also shattered a way of
thinking about God and humanity that had little to do with the Bible.
Martin Luther was a profound student of the Bible. He studied it in
detail and wrote commentaries on many books of the Bible. And in
the course of that study he discovered that what the church had

been teaching for centuries was simply wrong. Luther was able to penetrate centuries of encrusted theological tradition and get to the heart of the matter — which means that he was able to rediscover the truly radical nature of biblical faith, as taught by Saint Paul and Saint Augustine.

The Reformation was in this sense a conservative revolution, a revolution that reached back into the past to rediscover treasures that had been lost. The most radical revolutions in history have been conservative in that sense. Once the foundation has been rediscovered, however, newness can happen. Without the foundation, which in the Bible is the doctrine of justification, we would be attempting to build a house that would have to float in the air. This describes a great deal of recent theology. It looks shiny and new, but it has no depth and no ability to give us insight into the human situation. Such foundationless theology merely skips across the surface, like a stone that has been sent skipping across the surface of a pond of water. Such theology, like popular psychology, may be something to hang on to momentarily, but it has no staying power, no ability to lead us into the truth about ourselves, the world, or God.

The theology of Martin Luther, because it is solidly rooted in the Bible *and* in reality, the way life in the world is, is a theology of liberation in a double sense. First, Luther teaches us that we are set free from self-concern. The biblical doctrine of justification tells us that we are deeply cherished by the one who created us; therefore we need not fear what will happen to us when we die. We will be in heaven with Christ. Second, since we are set free from ourselves, we are now free for our neighbors and for the good earth. In Luther's terms, we are free to be little Christs to our neighbors and the earth. Four hundred years later, Dietrich Bonhoeffer, a student of Luther's theology, defined Jesus as "the man for others." As disciples of Jesus, we also are set free to be "for others."

The burden is not placed on us to create heaven on earth; God alone will create a new heaven and a new earth. Our vocation is much more modest. Our task, to quote Douglas John Hall (another contemporary student of Luther), is to be stewards of life in the kingdom of death, that is, to have a passion for life in a world that is in love with death. We are free to enjoy the beauty of the creation, free to relish every day, free even to enter into the dark places of our individual and collective lives without fear, knowing that the light of the world is already there before us. We are free even to fail, to make mistakes, to be imperfect. This isn't the freedom of a bull in a china shop but the freedom of sons and daughters who know how deeply we are loved. It is the freedom of people who know how to live imaginatively and creatively and who take great delight in doing so.

Because we always have the tendency to settle into old ways of thinking and acting, even when they are unproductive and harmful, the Reformation is never over. The church, moreover, is forever tempted to become an object of its own devotion, when its real task is to point beyond itself to Christ. And we can go about this work of reformation joyously, knowing that it ultimately doesn't depend on us and our efforts. We instead are participating in the much greater work of the Spirit of Christ. The Spirit alone will bring what we do to fruition.

For Further Reading

Bainton, Roland. *Here I Stand*. New York: Meridian, 1995. (The 1955 movie version of Bainton's biography is also available.)

Forde, Gerhard. *Where God Meets Man*. Minneapolis: Augsburg Publishing House, 1972.

_____. *Justification by Faith*. Philadelphia: Fortress Press, 1982.

_____. *On Being a Theologian of the Cross*. Grand Rapids: William B. Eerdmans Publishing Company, 1997.

_____. *Theology Is for Proclamation*. Minneapolis: Fortress Press, 1990.

Gritsch, Eric, and Robert Jenson. *Lutheranism*. Philadelphia: Fortress Press, 1976.

Kittelson, James. *Luther the Reformer*. Minneapolis: Augsburg Publishing House, 1986.

O'Neill, Judith. *Martin Luther*. Minneapolis: Lerner Publications Co., and Cambridge: Cambridge Univ. Press, 1979.

Endnotes

1. George W. Forell, "They Told What Had Happened on the Road," *Dialog* 33/ 2 (Spring 1994), p. 134.

2. *The Large Catechism of Martin Luther*, trans. Robert H. Fischer (Philadelphia: Fortress Press, 1959), p. 9.

3. Karl Barth, *Church Dogmatics* 4/1 (Edinburgh: T&T Clark, 1956), p. 7.

4. Alister E. McGrath, *Iustitia Dei: A History of the Christian Doctrine of Justification* (2 volumes; Cambridge: Cambridge Univ. Press, 1995).

5. James M. Kittelson, *Luther the Reformer* (Minneapolis: Augsburg Publishing House, 1986), pp. 32-33.

6. Kittelson, *Luther*, p. 37.

7. Roland Bainton, *Here I Stand: A Life of Martin Luther* (Nashville: Abingdon Press, 1950), p. 41.

8. Judith O'Neill, *Martin Luther* (Minneapolis: Lerner Publications Co., and Cambridge: Cambridge Univ. Press, 1979), p. 17.

9. O'Neill, *Luther*, p. 17.

10. There is evidence that, in fact, the church door was made of copper. In that case, the door could not have been used as a bulletin board. In any case, there was a wooden board used for such purposes near the Wittenberg castle church. See H. G. Haile, *Luther: An Experiment in Biography* (New York: Doubleday, 1980).

11. *Luther's Works*, vol. 31 (Philadelphia: Fortress Press, 1957), p. 25.

12. This is a paraphrase of Niebuhr's actual words. I can no longer trace the actual quotation.

13. Auden wrote: "Every crook will argue, 'I like committing crimes. God likes forgiving them. Really the world is admirably arranged.'" From *For the Time Being: A Christmas Oratorio*, in *Collected Poems* (ed. E. Mendelson; New York: Vintage Books, 1976), p. 394.

14. *The Large Catechism of Martin Luther*, p. 76.

15. O'Neill, *Luther*, p. 27.

16. The word "bull" comes from the Latin *bulla*, which was the lead seal attached to a papal letter.

17. O'Neill, *Luther*, p. 30.

18. O'Neill, *Luther*, p. 32.

19. *Luther's Works*, vol. 45 (Philadelphia: Fortress Press, 1962), p. 71.

20. *The Martin Luther Christmas Book*, trans. Roland H. Bainton (Philadelphia: Fortress Press, 1984), p. 22.

21. For more about the place of Mary in Christian theology, see Jaroslav Pelikan, *Mary through the Centuries* (New Haven: Yale Univ. Press, 1996).

22. Bainton, *Here I Stand*, p. 290.

23. Bainton, *Here I Stand*, pp. 295-296.

24. Two notorious examples are Luther's writings on the Jews and his tract on the Peasants' War.

    In 1523 he had written *That Jesus Christ Was Born a Jew*, in which he argued that Jews should be dealt with in a humanitarian way. In 1543, however, just three years before his death, he wrote *On the Jews and Their Lies* (English translation by Martin H. Bertram, in *Luther's Works*, American Edition, vol. 47 [Philadelphia: Fortress Press, 1971], 121-306). No defense can be made of this document, especially in light of the Holocaust and the fact that the Nazis made use of Luther's views to justify their "final solution." We can, however, attempt to understand Luther's views in the context of the situation in Europe and, more specifically, in Germany 500 years ago. By the early 1200s, Jews had been forbidden to pursue the professions in many parts of Europe and were thereby forced to become bankers and lenders, the only areas of employment open to them. By the 1500s, pogroms against the Jews had become commonplace in England, Spain, France, and Germany, which forced the Jewish population in Europe to migrate toward present-day Poland and Russia. At the time of the Reformation, the great humanist Erasmus of Rotterdam could boast that France was free of Jews. Luther's view, to his credit, was a bit more nuanced than the views of others of his time. By 1523, he was known as a friend of the Jews, because of his insistence (uncommon at the time) that Jesus was Jewish. And in the Wittenberg Hymnal of 1544,

Luther made it quite clear that it was not the Jews who crucified Jesus; the guilt, rather, resides with Christians.

> *Our great sin and sore misdeed*
> *Jesus, the true Son of God, the Cross has nailed.*
> *Thus you poor Judas, as well as all the Jews*
> *we may not upbraid inimically,*
> *for the guilt is ours.*

For more on this topic, see Heiko A. Oberman, *Luther: Man between God and the Devil* (Yale Univ. Press, 1982), 289-297, and Bernhard Lohse, *Martin Luther's Theology* (Fortress Press, 1999), pp. 336-345.

Luther's attitude toward the German peasants during and after the Peasants' War of 1524-1525 led by Thomas Müntzer, seems to us inexcusably harsh. Again, context is important for understanding what was going on. The peasants were fighting against real oppression. In a time when hunger and disease were ravaging the countryside, landlords, who had lost many workers, made virtual slaves of those workers who remained on their land. When the countess of Lüpfen compelled her peasants to pick strawberries for a great banquet she was planning, they rebelled. The rebellion spread little by little. Thomas Müntzer urged them on, proclaiming that the kingdom of God was at hand and that the bullets fired at them by the princes would be harmless to them. Unfortunately, the peasant army was massacred at the Battle of Frankenhausen. Müntzer was found hiding in bed and was executed. The peasants, who had at one time supported Luther, now jeered at him and threatened him for not supporting their rebellion. Luther, like many others at the time, was terrified of rebellion and the anarchy it would bring. Europe was already being terrorized by the plague and there was precious little to create order in society. For more see Kittelson, *Luther the Reformer*, 189-192, and Bainton, *Here I Stand*, pp. 268-285.

25. Bainton, *Here I Stand*, p. 304.

26. O'Neill, *Luther*, p. 48.

27. See Gerhard Forde, *Where God Meets Man: Luther's Down-to-Earth Approach to the Gospel* (Minneapolis: Augsburg Publishing House, 1972).

28. Forde, *Where God Meets Man*, pp. 7-8.

29. Howard Zinn, *A People's History of the United States: 1492-Present* (New York: Harper Perennial, 1995).

30. See note 2 above.

31. "For the Lord will rise up as on Mount Perazim, he will rage as in the valley of Gibeon: to do his deed — strange is his deed! And to work his work — alien is his work!"

32. "Truly, you are a God who hides himself, O God of Israel, the Savior."

33. Kittelson, *Luther*, p. 93.

34. Harry McClintock wrote and recorded "Big Rock Candy Mountain" in 1928:

> *One evening as the sun went down, and the jungle fire*
> *was burning,*
> *Down the track came a hobo hiking, and he said, "Boys,*
> *I'm not turning,*
> *I'm headed for a land that's far away, beside the crys-*
> *tal fountain,*
> *So come with me, we'll go and see, the big rock candy*
> *mountain.*
>
> *"In the big rock candy mountain, there's a land that's*
> *fair and bright,*
> *Where the handouts grow on bushes, and you sleep out*
> *every night,*
> *Where the boxcars all are empty, and the sun shines*
> *every day,*
> *On the birds and bees and the cigarette trees,*
> *The lemonade springs where the bluebird sings,*
> *In the big rock candy mountain.*
>
> *"In the big rock candy mountain, all the cops have*
> *wooden legs,*
> *And the bulldogs all have rubber teeth, and the hens*
> *lay soft-boiled eggs.*
> *The farmers' trees are full of fruit, and the barns are*
> *full of hay,*
> *Well I'm bound to go where there ain't no snow,*
> *Where the rain don't flow and the wind don't blow,*
> *In the big rock candy mountain.*
>
> *"In the big rock candy mountain, you never change your*
> *socks,*
> *And the little streams of alcohol come a tricklin' down*
> *the rocks.*
> *The brakemen have to tip their hats, and the railroad*
> *bulls are blind,*

There's a lake of stew and of whiskey, too,
You can paddle all around 'em in a big canoe,
In the big rock candy mountain.

"In the big rock candy mountain, the jails are made of
tin,
And you can walk right out again, as soon as you are
in.
There ain't no short-handled shovels, no axes or their
picks.
I'm going to stay where ya sleep all day,
Where they hung the jerk who invented work
In the big rock candy mountain.

"I'll see you all this comin' fall,
In the big rock candy mountain."

35. Kittelson, *Luther*, p. 286.

36. John Walsh, *Strange Harp, Strange Symphony: The Life of Francis Thompson* (New York: Hawthorn Books, 1967), p. 64.

37. The material on Francis Thompson's life is from an Internet article by Beth Randall, © 1996.

38. See Saint Augustine, *Confessions*, book 4, section 4: "But you were present, immediately at the back of those who flee from you, at once both 'God of vengeances' (Psalm 93:1) and fount of mercies: you turn us to yourself in wonderful ways" (trans. Henry Chadwick [Oxford: Oxford Univ. Press, 1991], p. 56).

39. The phrase is borrowed from British writer Charles Williams, friend of C. S. Lewis and J. R. R. Tolkien, "And Troilus 'undergoes an entire subversion of his whole experience' " (Humphrey Carpenter, *The Inklings* [San Francisco: HarperCollins, 1997], p. 90).

40. James Luther Adams, *On Being Human Religiously* (Boston: Beacon Press, 1976), p. 96.

41. Douglas John Hall, *Lighten Our Darkness: Towards an Indigenous Theology of the Cross* (rev. ed.; Lima, Ohio: Academic Renewal Press, 2001), p. 153. "The theology of the cross is the detailing of an entrance into the nihil, an abandonment that is just as negating, but which nonetheless meets in that void the creative Word — the Word that creates *ex nihilo*."

42. Reinhold Niebuhr, *The Irony of American History* (New York: Scribner, 1952).

43. From the Augsburg Confession, in *The Book of Concord*, ed. Robert Kolb and Timothy J. Wengert (Minneapolis: Fortress Press, 2000), p. 42.

44. *The Book of Concord*, p. 469.

45. Edward Schillebeeckx, *The Mission of the Church* (London: Sheed and Ward, 1973), p. 45.

46. Karl Rahner, *The Christian of the Future* (New York: Herder and Herder, 1967), p. 89.

47. Paul Tillich, "Behold, I Am Doing a New Thing," in *The Essential Tillich*, ed. F. Forrester Church (Chicago: Univ. of Chicago Press, 1999), p. 281.

48. See Hall, *Lighten Our Darkness*.

49. Forde, *Where God Meets Man*, p. 118.

50. Forde, *Where God Meets Man*, pp. 124-125.

51. Karl Barth, "*Fiat Iustitia*," in *Karl Barth: Theologian of Freedom* (ed. Clifford Green; Minneapolis: Fortress Press, 1991), p. 255.

52. Paul Lehmann, *Ethics in a Christian Context* (New York: Harper & Row, 1963).

53. Douglas John Hall, *The Stewardship of Life in the Kingdom of Death* (Grand Rapids, Mich.: Wm. B. Eerdmans Publishing Co., 1985).

54. Martin Luther, "Two Kinds of Righteousness," in Timothy Lull, ed., *Martin Luther's Basic Theological Writings* (Minneapolis: Fortress Press, 1989), p. 157.

55. Dietrich Bonhoeffer, *Discipleship* (Minneapolis: Fortress Press, 2001), p. 62.

56. Bonhoeffer, *Discipleship*, p. 64.

57. Jürgen Moltmann, *The Passion for Life* (Philadelphia: Fortress Press, 1978), pp. 25-26.

58. Moltmann, *The Passion for Life*, p. 26.